What is a Witch?

A Witch stands between the worlds of physical being and spiritual being, communicating with plants and animals, the energies of Nature, the spirit entities of other worlds, and the spirits of ancestors or the recently deceased.

She respects the world and sees herself in harmony with her surroundings and with her fellow beings. The changing of the seasons, the scents in the air, the comings and goings of animals, birds, fish, insects, and reptiles are all observed and understood as part of a vast integrated pattern of life.

She is the shaman, medicine person, healer, herbalist, and spiritualist found in both ancient and modern societies, linking the past, the present, and the future.

About the Author

Raised in a family tradition of three generations, Ann Moura writes of her heritage as a Green Witch, passing along to a new generation lessons learned from her Brazilian mother and grandmother of Celtic-Iberian descent. Their understanding of folk magics and Craft concepts included the often-repeated Rules of Conduct, ancient deities, spiritism, herbal spells, candle magics, reincarnation belief, calling upon the Elementals, and an understanding of The Power.

Moura focuses on a practice of Witchcraft that includes working with the energies and spirits of Nature, with the Elementals, and with the Goddess and God of Nature. She holds B.A. and M.A. degrees in history, and enjoys writing, poetry, drawing, painting, and gardening. Married, with two grown children raised in the Craft, Ann writes about the Craft from the perspective of her personal experience, family training, and community awareness. She teaches classes on her family tradition, presents workshops at Pagan Festivals, does book signings and tarot readings, writes articles for Pagan online newsletters, does radio interviews, and attends publishing and New Age-oriented conventions.

To Write to the Author

If you wish to contact the author or would like more information about this book, please write to the author in care of Llewellyn Worldwide and we will forward your request. Both the author and publisher appreciate hearing from you and learning of your enjoyment of this book and how it has helped you. Llewellyn Worldwide cannot guarantee that every letter written to the author can be answered, but all will be forwarded. Write to:

Ann Moura
c/o Llewellyn Worldwide
P.O. Box 64383, Dept. 0-7387-0343-5
St. Paul, MN 55164-0383, U.S.A.

Please enclose a self-addressed stamped envelope for reply, or $1.00 to cover costs. If outside U.S.A., enclose international postal reply coupon.

Many of Llewellyn's authors have websites with additional information and resources. For more information, please visit our website at http://www.llewellyn.com.

Witchcraft
an Alternative Path

Ann Moura

2003
Llewellyn Publications
St. Paul, Minnesota 55164-0383, U.S.A.

FIRST EDITION
First Printing, 2003

Book interior design and editing by Connie Hill
Cover design by Lisa Novak
Cover images © 2002 by Digital Vision

Library of Congress Cataloging-in-Publication Data
Moura, Ann
  Witchcraft : an alternative path / Ann Moura (Aoumiwl) — 1st ed.
     p.   cm.
  Includes bibliographical references (p.) and index.
  ISBN 0-7387-0343-5
  1. Witchcraft—Handbooks, manuals, etc.   I. Title.
  BF1566.A57   2003
299—dc21   2002044418

Llewellyn Worldwide does not participate in, endorse, or have any authority or responsibility concerning private business transactions between our authors and the public.
  All mail addressed to the author is forwarded but the publisher cannot, unless specifically instructed by the author, give out an address or phone number.
  Any Internet references contained in this work are current at publication time, but the publisher cannot guarantee that a specific location will continue to be maintained. Please refer to the publisher's website for links to authors' websites and other sources.

Llewellyn Publications
A Division of Llewellyn Worldwide, Ltd.
P.O. Box 64383, Dept. 0-7387-0343-5
St. Paul, MN 55164-0383, U.S.A.
www.llewellyn.com

Printed in the United States of America

Dedication

To the Old Religion and all those
who seek the Old Ways.

Also by Ann Moura

Dancing Shadows: The Roots of Western Religious Beliefs
   (as Aoumiel)

Green Witchcraft: Folk Magic, Fairy Lore & Herb Craft

Green Witchcraft II: Balancing Light and Shadow

Green Witchcraft III: The Manual

Origins of Modern Witchcraft

Green Magic: The Sacred Connection to Nature

Contents

Acknowledgments

Many thanks to all the wonderful people at Llewellyn who have helped to make this book come into being, and especially to Nancy Mostad for her continued encouragement. Recognition is certainly due to my family for putting up with my mole-like habits when writing a manuscript, and to my wonderfully considerate husband (thanks for the computer and for keeping it updated!), and to the friends who bring me back to the real world with tea—yes, that's you Kim, Sonne, Lisa, and Willa. Also, many thanks to Miranda for her support and promoting of my work, to Willa and Carl for their generous hospitality, to Helen and Kodi for bringing my books to so many festivals, and definitely to that organizational sorceress, Ann Marie, for her warm enthusiasm and kind invitations to Pagan festivals and events. My warmest blessings go out to each and every one.

Introduction to Witchcraft

What Is a Witch?

The word "Witch" carries a lot of impressions to the average person. Some are negative and some are positive, but all the images that come to mind speak in one way or another to a sense of awe and magical powers. There are many misconceptions about what a Witch is and is not, and even what terms to use when discussing Witches. The entertainment industry has sought ways to distinguish between male and female Witches, using Witch for females, and varying between warlock (Scottish for "an oath-breaker," but Norse for "a male magician"), wizard, magician, magus, and sorcerer for males. Yet in actual practice, "Witch" is the word used for both males and females. Popular culture has added all kinds of nonsense to the description of Witches, from twitchy noses to giddy pyro-technics, but this creates a false perception, a facade that serves more to illustrate the difference between entertainment and spirituality, between fantasy and reality, than to demonstrate the substance of Witchcraft.

Witches have always been part of human societies, with different names or titles depending on the time period or location, but identifiable as a people who have a heightened sense of Nature and the ability to access the interconnection of all life on the planet. These people study herbs, the stars, the seasons, and animal behavior. They stand between the worlds of physical being and spiritual being, communicating with plants and animals, the energies of Nature, the spirit entities of other worlds, and the spirits of ancestors or the recently deceased. They respect their world and see themselves in harmony with their surroundings and with their fellow beings, and they have developed a sense of awareness for their environment. The changing of the seasons, the scents in the air, the comings and goings of animals, birds, fish, insects, and reptiles are all observed and understood as part of a vast integrated pattern of life. They are the shamans, medicine people, healers, herbalists, and spiritualists found in both ancient and modern societies, linking the past, the present, and the future.

The Witch is one who is attuned to the ebb and flow of this overall life pattern; one who bridges the worlds of the seen and the unseen; and one who follows a moral ethic that ensures that personal balance is maintained in all areas of life. All of this formed the Natural approach to spirituality known as the Old Religion. In the early centuries of Christian establishment, people who did not convert and conform to the orthodoxy created by the Catholic Church were persecuted under various names: heretic, pagan, Witch. From the start, there were many variations of Christian observances, and those whose beliefs differed from the regionally dominant orthodoxy were called heretics, while those who dwelled in rural areas and continued to practice the ancient agricultural and fertility rites were scornfully ridiculed as bumpkins and ignorant rustics, *pagani*, from which comes the word "Pagan." The counselors, herbalists, healers, shamans, naturalists, midwives, and spiritualists of former times were now lumped in with the heretics and Pagans as Witches. Of course, not everyone called a Witch actually was one, but the accusation was frequently used against nonconformists, independent thinkers, wealthy but socially isolated people, or landowners with rivals. Today, however, a Witch is someone who has returned to the ancestral spiritual concepts, of being one with, and part of, the Earth and the Universe, and bringing this awareness into the daily routine by living a magical life and revering the ancient deities of Nature.

Today's Witch is the inheritor of the Old Religion, revitalized and updated for modern society to be a spiritual path that opens a person's psychic perception to embrace the Divine Spirit residing in Nature and the Universe. Witches may specialize in those areas of the Craft that appeal to them, be it herbalism, spirit communication, divination, spell crafting, astrology, healing, weather working, crystal work, or other such fields. Many modern Witches prefer to be called Wiccan (pronounced as *Wik'kan)*, emphasizing their spiritual heritage. But even this medieval English word, whose etymology could be derived from the terms for wise one, gateway, willow, or even alive, was in its own time pronounced as *Weetchie*, thus leading to the modern word, "Witch."

The term "Wiccan" is often used to avoid the negative imagery of the Witches of fairy tales and scary stories, yet these tales are part of the heritage of religious persecution that continued for many centuries in Europe until only relatively recent times. Of course not all storybook Witches are portrayed as evil. There are stories of good Witches, like Glinda from *The Wizard of Oz*; protective fairy godmothers, as in *Sleeping Beauty*; Witches who aid the heroine of the story, as in *The Three Spinners*; and Witches who help damsels in distress while ensuring the seasons pass in proper succession, such as *Old Mother Hulda*. Even Chaucer's *Canterbury Tales* include that of a knight wedding a Witch, who taught him that women cherish their independence ("The Wife of Bath"). Some stories demonstrate that the good or evil of all people, including Witches comes from within, and so there are good and evil Witches in the stories of Oz as well as in the Harry Potter books. It is important to realize that merely being a Witch does not make a person good or evil, for these are qualities harbored and nurtured by individuals, no matter what their spirituality, but Witches are especially aware of being personally responsible for their actions.

In Witchcraft, the unity of life on Earth is sometimes referred to as *Gaia*. This term means that the life force of the planet is an integral part of everything on the Earth, so that the Witch is part of the lifeform called Earth, or Mother Earth. The cycles of life for the planet are observed, honored, and reflected in the microcosm of each being, as well as in the macrocosm of the Universe. Because everyone and everything on Earth is part of Gaia, the Witch respects the other creatures of the Earth and avoids disturbing their habitat, seeking instead to live in harmony with other life forms. This means that while animals and plants may be eaten, the Witch takes only what is needed so that the species may reproduce and continue. Even in taking herbs for magical work, only one from a clump of plants, or only a portion of a plant is used. This way, the integrity of the species is maintained, with the rest left intact to continue to grow and reseed. Hunting, fishing, logging, and changing the landscape through farming and building are part of the requirements of modern living, for all life feeds on life and impacts the environment in one way or another, but the Witch walks with care on the Earth, working with conservation, clean-up, and recycling efforts to minimize damage or to repair the delicate balance of the ecosystem.

The energy of earthquakes, tornadoes, volcanoes, and floods are respected as evidence of the power of the Elemental extensions of the Divine into Earth, Air, Fire, and Water, and prudence is exercised in those areas prone to these conditions. Some Witches may work magic to avoid provoking these energies in their areas, to utilize these energies in adding power to spells, or to direct them away from habitations. The Witch cares about the ecology of the Earth and seeks to avoid the reckless destruction of the fragile environment. Many are active in recycling and clean-up efforts, and most support conservation in one manner or another. The sciences are embraced as knowledge and wisdom from Nature, the Universe, and the Divine. Most Witches place great emphasis on widespread education, with the hope that people will come to understand that the vast population of the Earth is interdependent both upon one another and upon the environment for continued survival, and that what people in one area do has an effect on people in other areas through sea, air, and energy currents.

Some Beliefs of the Witch

Witches tend to be at peace with the world, accepting of changes in the seasons and in life, for the one constant in Nature is change. There is a sense of kinship between the Practitioner and all of the life forms of Earth, so that there is respect for other peoples and their ways of life, as well as for the animal, vegetable, and mineral life forms. The differences between life forms are acknowledged as manifesting the immense capacity for diversity of the Divine, and it is understood that everyone is a distinct individual, yet all are connected through the spirit of Nature, the indwelling spirit of the Goddess and the God. The *Natural Witch*—one whose focus is with the Divine in Nature and working directly with the energies of Nature—is often *Pantheistic,* meaning that the Divine is seen as dwelling within everything, and *Animistic,* meaning that everything is seen as alive with the indwelling Spirit of the Divine. This makes it easy for the Witch to communicate with those things that other people might ordinarily believe to be inanimate objects. Even stones, crystals, and gems are believed by the Witch to contain spirit entities or energies, making these objects alive and able to aid in spell work and other magics. Since the Spirit of the Divine also resides within every living thing, the Witch considers that everyone is interrelated through the Divine with everything on the Earth and throughout the Universe. This vision of spiritual unity means that the Witch is at one with, and therefore is, the Earth, the Universe, and the Divine.

In Witchcraft, the term "Divine" refers to a duality in the universal power that is the Deity source of spiritual energy, making the Divine aspected as Goddess and God, and also as Both. The Goddess is often called the Lady, while the God is called the Lord, but each has been known throughout the world by many names. These names for the Divine are often simply nouns, aspects, or perceived attributes stated in an ancient language, and generally translatable to such things as Great Goddess and Great God, Lady and Lord, Great Mother and Great Father, Abundance, Power, Beneficent, Wisdom, Ancient One, and so forth. This is why in Witchcraft there are many different names for the Goddess and the God, and Witches choose the names that appeal to them— that they can personally relate to—or use no names, but only Lady and Lord or Goddess and God. The aspect of Both is also known as the Divine Androgyne, and has been represented as the Great All, with the Egyptian deity image of Atum being revered at Karnac until the temple was legally closed by the Christian Senate of Rome in the fourth century C.E. (*Common Era* or *Current Era*, used by many historians in lieu of the Christian A.D.). In modern India, the ancient aspect of the Divine Androgyne is one of Shiva, called Shiva Ardhanari (*Shiva, Half Male and Half Female*), as a literal image with one side masculine and the other side feminine from head to toe. This depiction initially led some Europeans to assume that Shiva was female, when actually Shiva (easily recognized as the figure dancing within a circle of flames) is male. His other half is Shakti, identifiable as Parvati and Kali, is female, but together, as Ardhanari, they are One. In ancient Rome, this same androgenous quality was ascribed to Mercury, the messenger of the Gods, and humans who were born androgynes were revered as having a sacred connection to the duality (maleness and femaleness) of the Divine. Today, fully 10 percent of babies born in the United States alone are androgynes, but they are surgically altered in infancy to be one sex or the other, as chosen by their parents and doctors.

The personal relationship with the Divine, and the sense of oneness with the Earth and the Universe, allows the Witch to feel comfortable and secure with pursuing the interests and lifestyle that brings personal joy and contentment, knowing that the Goddess and the God will be close at hand to provide whatever assistance is needed. From this concept comes the expression of *Perfect Love and Perfect Trust* found so often in Witchcraft rituals. The idea is that the individual Witch accepts the love of the Goddess and the God, and puts his or her trust in Them.

Freedom of the individual and personal responsibility are key aspects of Witchcraft. Creeds and liturgies may be created as needed or desired, for the magic will naturally flow with the acceptance of oneness with the All and with self-responsibility in our living. Witches do not believe in an inherent evil or that humanity is born into a condition of sinfulness, and so there is no need for forgiveness or redemption. Being human is natural and proper for the species, and that is part of the cycle of life. How people choose to live their lives is where personal responsibility comes into play. Hence, evil exists as symptoms within the individual—loneliness, lack of self-worth, fears, self-abasement, isolation—that are reflected outward in behavior patterns, emotional, or mental states of agitation, anger, hatred, and hostility toward the self or others. Attend to the cause, and the behavior is alleviated, but this attention must ultimately come from within. No one can make another person feel self-esteem, unity, or love. Indeed, without love of self, there cannot be love of another—it takes the individual's self-confidence and feeling secure about who that person is that allows room for feelings of love and security for other people. The "Charge of the Goddess" by Charles Leland, amended by Gerald Gardner and Doreen Valiente, offers the key mystery that unless a person can find internally what is sought, that person will never find it externally.

The basic ethic of the Craft has been stated in many ways as the principle of harming none. Even the most familiar ethic, called the "Witches' Rede," created by Gerald Gardner and Doreen Valiente, exists in several variations, including this traditional one:

> *Bide to the Witches' Law ye must; In perfect love and perfect trust.*
> *Eight words the Witches' Rede fulfill; An' it harm none, do as ye will.*
> *What ye send forth returns to thee; so ever mind the Rule of Three.*
> *Follow this with mind and heart; and merry ye meet and merry ye part.*

The main rule is to harm none, with the primary belief that the energy a person sends outwardly attracts like energy back, in equal amount or three times the original amount depending on the tradition. Thus, by focusing on negativity, a person will experience negative energies simply through attracting them. *Harm none* also applies to the practitioner of the Craft, so a person must be careful with the energy sent into the surrounding environment.

A variation of Witchcraft is shamanism, in the prehistoric and aboriginal sense of being a person who communes with spirits, works to heal the sick, and guides the dying in their passage from this life. The traditional path of the Shaman usually involves a vision quest undertaken in a wilderness area and includes several days of fasting, meditation within the confines of a circle, seeking a totem guide, and even drawing close to death. Because of the physical dangers, this path should not be approached without the careful preparation and guidance of a master.

Other beliefs of the Old Religion include spiritism and reincarnation. With spiritism, the Witch is contacting and working with the spirit realm, and could be communicating with those who have passed on, the ancestors, or the consciousness of other beings from other worlds and planes of existence (such as the astral). Thus, spiritism can involve a reunion with deceased loved ones or communion with what are considered angelic or Otherworld entities. Reincarnation is the belief that the cycle of life on Earth—as evidenced, for example, in the growth of plants from their seeds, their harvest, their reseeding, their repose over winter, and their resurgence at spring—is reflected in the passage of the soul from birth through life, into death, repose, and a return to the physical plane through rebirth into a new body. Thus the body is the avatar of the human spirit, the symbiotic material form through which spiritual consciousness is carried in the physical world. When physical life is completed, the spirit passes from the body, and the body then decomposes and returns to the basic elements of its construction. The spirit, meanwhile, moves through the death passage into Underworld, the realm of the God in his aspect of Lord of Shadows.

Most mythologies see the Underworld as a two-fold location, with an area for rest and an area for activity. In Witchcraft, the place of rest and repose is Shadowland. It is here that the spirit is soothed and relieved of the stress accumulated during the life phase so that the spirit is re-energized, regaining balance and peace. From Shadowland, the refreshed spirit may move on to Summerland—a sort of Elysium Fields or Paradise—where the spirit may remain as long as desired, experiencing harmony, joy, and bliss. Here the spirit may contemplate personal growth and decide on what further physical experience may be needed for spiritual development. The spirit then chooses when and where to return to the physical world to learn, to grow, or to experiment with the options offered by corporeal life. Reincarnation results, and only rarely does the spirit recall previous incarnations or the spirit existence in great detail, but it does happen more frequently in smaller snippets of remembrance. There have been recorded cases, usually treated as mere oddities, of total recollection of past life experience. It appears that a spirit may occasionally choose to return to physical life rapidly, perhaps without thorough rest or consideration, or with the deliberate desire to retain memories which may be offered as evidence to others of the reality of reincarnation.

The creative forces of Nature are revered, with the God and the Goddess being the Universal Energies and Materials from which comes all existence, equal and omnipresent, found throughout the Earth and the Universe, and all that dwell therein. Because it is the Spiral Dance of Rebirth that brings the spirit back to the Divine source of existence in the Goddess and the God, reincarnation and communication with spirits are generally accepted parts of the religion, and the Elementals of Earth, Air, Fire, and Water help the Witch in magical work whether viewed as independent entities or as extensions of the immanent Divine.

Since knowledge is the gift of the Goddess and the God, the Witch may draw closer to them through the learning that takes place during many lives on Earth. Magic is a means of connecting with the Divine in working with energy to accomplish a goal, and this magic is a natural part of life for the practicing Witch. Consciousness may be altered through visualization, music, dance, meditation, and ritual to better commune with the Divine and effect the magic. Through an evolving or ritual dedication, that communication opens permanently, so that contact with the Divine in Nature is readily achieved through inner stillness and balance. Most importantly, the Witch feels the connection with the Divine, and when invoking the Elementals, the God, or the Goddess, has every expectation of a response. This means that communication with the deity is not mere form or ritual, but active and vital with an anticipation of sensory manifestation.

The Goddess and the God

Immanence, interconnection, and community are three core principles of Witchcraft. Because the God and the Goddess are manifested in all life, all existence is connected to be one living cosmos. The focus is on the growth of the whole through care for the Earth, the environment, and one another. The mythology of the Lord and the Lady revolves around two themes in the Wheel of the Year—that of the life cycle of the God, and that of fertility and the passage of the seasons. Thus, the "sacrificed god" motif can be found in the Corn (Wheat) Cycle, wherein the God willingly gives his life-force into the crops in a sacred marriage with the Earth so that humanity may be sustained. This is one of the actions in various mythologies (Cybele and Attis, Isis and Osiris) that serve to relate the Divine to human life and the passage from life through death to new life. Further self-sacrifice on the part of the God occurs with the Vine (or Fruit) Cycle, wherein the God passes his spirit into a crop that is harvested and fermented into wine, cider, or whiskey (Dionysos, Bacchus, John Barleycorn). In ancient times it was believed that the celebrant, imbued with the spirit of the God, was capable of divination, prophecy, and ecstasy, bringing the Divine into a personal esoteric experience. Today's wine festivals in Europe are vestiges of these ancient rites of Dionysos or Bacchus, but there are also beer, mead, and barleycorn (for whiskey) festivals with ancient roots in deity communion.

The Triple Goddess is seen in her three aspects of Maiden, Mother, and Crone (Matron), and has as her consort the Horned God. This aspect of the God shows him as Creator (Greenman), Lord of the Animals (Wildwood), and Destroyer (Hunter). The Triple God is seen as Youth, Greenman, and Sage, and is usually depicted with deer or stag antlers to emphasize his role in the Earth's fertility as well as that of Nature's wildlife. Since all Nature has both positive and negative aspects, and to be reborn one must first die, the Goddess is seen as both womb in her form as Mother and tomb in her form as Crone, yet both are the same. Death is the natural passage to new life and is neither feared nor considered an evil. With Nature there are both pleasant and harsh aspects, but this is all part of the reality of the energy that flows in the Earth, the Universe, and the beings of the Earth. The transition of the spirit through incarnations is not feared, but understood and accepted as natural, for life is eternal, and all spirits are immortal.

Since a Witch can choose those names for the Divine that have a personal appeal, the option is there to embrace an entire pantheon of ancient deities. Some Witches follow a precise pantheon, using only the deities and mythologies of a particular pre-Christian society, such as the Norse, Germanic, Teutonic, Saxon, Celtic, Egyptian, Sumerian, Indian, Thracian, Greek, Roman, Etruscan, Welsh, Finnish, Aboriginal American, African, and so forth. Others choose to intermingle the deities that appeal to them, and even those Witches who profess to adhere to one pantheon will often, and perhaps inadvertently, include a deity that had even in ancient times transcended geographic and cultural locations. Mixing pantheons was the norm rather than the unusual in ancient times as cultures intermingled, with Rome being famous for the variety of gods and goddesses having shrines and temples reflecting the deities of the lands brought into the Empire. The fact that these different deities are easily adaptable and compatible stems from their heritage as universal archetypes. The myths may vary, but the themes are the same, so the same image of the God or Goddess may be identified by different names in diverse cultures.

Today, most Witches select their personal images for the Divine to match those aspects they relate to most. Thus, a Witch's altar may have Cernunnos and Cerridwen, Hecate and Herne, Poseidon and Yemana, Pan and Rhiannon, and so forth. Appendix A lists some of the Gods and Goddesses typically honored by modern Witches. It is the archetypes represented in these aspects of the Divine that make a particular deity meaningful to the Witch, and yet there is a common thread so that, despite aspects, all the Gods are one God, and all the Goddesses are one Goddess, and together they both form the All.

The theme of both God and Goddess being One is seen in mythological androgyne motifs where male heroes, such as Heracles, go through a period of time dressed as females, or where a deity is depicted as both male and female, as with the Egyptian deity Atum and the Indian deity image of Shiva as Ardhanari. The concept of the Divine Androgyne is even found in the Biblical description of God in Genesis speaking in the plural during the creation, in which "man" is made in "our image" and as "both male and female." The idea of unity is so ancient that it has passed into the modern mainstream religions, although the significance of the words tends to be overlooked.

The Wheel of the Year Concept

Since the Divine Spirit that resides within each person is immortal, likewise are people naturally immortal, and mythologies function to demonstrate the cycle of life from incarnation and birth to death passage and new life. Reincarnation of the person through many lifetimes or simply the movement of the spirit from body into the living Earth is usually an aspect of the Witch's spirituality, with the soul purpose possibly determined prior to rebirth. But not all Witches believe in reincarnation so much as in a reunion with Mother Earth, which creates energy regions on the planet wherever spirits dwell in large numbers. These are often recognized as sacred or ancestral sites and places for meditative and spiritual retreats. The idea of the land being sacred is understandable in terms of the life essence of the people of the land returning to it for the benefit of their descendants. Spirits that unite with the land are seen as ensuring the fertility of the soil and the animals, bringing the rain and the fresh water, hearing the supplications of the descendants, offering their protection to their heirs, and accepting the honors their descendants do them through ancestor rituals.

The concept of life passage and the cycle of the year form the basis for the Witches' Sabbats and the accompanying archetypal mythologies, which may vary depending on the pantheon and the Tradition (Craft denomination). Despite alterations, the theme is of the basic flow of life centered around the phases of the Sun in a yearly succession. The methods of honoring the God and the Goddess during these times relate to the God bringing his energy into the grain of Mother Earth, and his spirit into the vine for life on Earth to be sustained. In older days, wine was drunk by everyone and was used to purify water, and so the fruit of the vine was vitally important to life. In a modern perspective, consider that it is now possible through genetic engineering to create one-crop-only plant seeds—seeds that will produce a crop whose own seeds are infertile. This is the deliberate destruction by humanity of the God's gift of fertility. The theme of the God is that it is his energy that breathes life into the seed and into the grain that grows from it, and thus into the fertile seeds produced by that grain for the next season. The spirit of the God entering into the vine was part of the ancient tradition of wine being the medium for the ecstatic experience of communion with the Divine, as with the maenads or bacchantes who reveled in drunkenness for Dionysos or Bacchus, and were considered sacred and protected from harm by the populace during their union with the God.

The bread and wine of Lughnassadh, Mabon, and the Simple Feast or Cakes and Wine of every Sabbat and Esbat ritual are the ancestral equivalent of the holy communion ritual practiced by mainstream churches. The difference lies in the expectation for the Witch that the food and beverage is imbued with the energy of the Divine, and that this energy is passed on in blessing to all of the participants. In the Catholic communion, the wine is believed to be literally transformed into blood, and the wafer into flesh—

both of which were consumed only by the officiating priest until Vatican II in the 1960s. Prior to this, the congregation did not receive the wine, and only received smaller wafers from a plate not lifted to receive Divine blessing, but merely set upon the altar—hence, the congregation was fed by the Church, but the representative of the Church was fed by the Divine. Today all the wafers are normally lifted and there is an option of everyone sharing a communion cup at the discretion of the presiding priest and the communicant. While most Protestant denominations follow a communion that allows the whole congregation to consume both the blessed beverage and slices of bread—either at the front of the church or passed through the pews in little individual glasses and slices of bread on trays—they do not believe that an actual transformation has taken place, hence this is only a symbolic ritual without an energizing taking place. The Cakes and Wine of the Witch, however, is more like the *puja* (offering) of Hinduism, in which Divine energy is passed into the sacred feast that is then drunk and eaten by the participants who draw into themselves the Divine essence in a personal union.

Another aspect of the Divine that is incorporated into the Turning of the Wheel of the Year is the acceptance and understanding that the Dark Aspects of the Goddess and the God keep the cycle of life in balance. They represent light, but they also represent shadow, so that while they bring life, they also take the individual through the death passage to enter into new life. Thus the God of fertility and self-sacrifice is also the Hunter, who gathers the dead to pass through the Crone Goddess who is also the Mother Goddess of fertility. The God and the Goddess also represent Incipience as the Youth and the Maiden, that period of commencement of life in which the freshness and possibilities of new beginnings is apparent.

The most sacred time of year for the Witch symbolizes the transition of Samhain, or Halloween (*Holy Eve*), when death is a passage to the new life revealed at Yule. The returning power of the Sun in the infant God, born of that same Goddess who afforded the death passage, shows her to be both the tomb and the womb. The three great mysteries of the religion are revealed in the Triple Aspect of the God as Sage, Father, and Son; the Triple Aspect of the Goddess as Maiden, Mother, and Crone; and the union of Tomb and Womb in the eternal cycle of immortal life. There is no neurotic need to search for some illusive "meaning of life" simply because the joy of life comes from living it without fear.

Witchcraft may address Nature through the Elemental energies of the soil, stones, and vegetation springing up from the ground, the wind, clouds, and freshness of the sky, the solar heat and light, and the fresh, mineral, and salted waters. But the Craft may also address Nature through the aspects of a Divine All that is both separate as Goddess and God, and unified as Both. Because the Goddess and the God are two halves of the same whole, their aspects or forms are interlinked and interchangeable: Father Sky and Mother Earth/Sky Goddess and Earth God; Sun and Moon; Triple Goddess and Wed to the Triple Goddess; Threefold God and Wed to the Threefold God; Lord and Lady of the Greenwood or Wild Wood; Lord of Abundance and Lady of Plenty; Queen of the Stars and King of the Universe; Creator and Creatrix, Spirit and Matter; Life and Passage; Cosmic Dancers of Energy and Matter, and many other such combinations. It is because of all the Divine attributes and aspects that the Elementals, even in a Witchcraft that functions purely as magical practice, still bring the Divine into the Craft through the connection of the emanating spirit and energy into material form. Thus the God is associated with the spiritual Air and animating Fire, while the Goddess is associated with the life-giving Water and physicality of Earth.

The Pentagram

The symbol most often associated with Witchcraft is the five-pointed star within a circle, called a pentagram. With one point at the top, the emblem may be said to resemble a person standing with head up, arms out at the sides and feet spread. Another meaning for this symbol is that it represents the four Elementals of Earth, Air, Fire, and Water in the arms and feet portion of the star, and Spirit in the head portion. Some add that communion with the Divine is at the center of the star. Rarely used as inverted, this symbol may in that position represent the Horned God, which is the God aspect of fertility, wilderness, and the Hunter who guides spirits to Underworld. Unfortunately, the inverted star is also used by Satanists, whose religion is basically a protest against Christianity. Witches do not have a devil, so there is no Satan, and they are not acting in protest against any other religion, but practicing the Old Religion that existed prior to Judaism, Christianity, and Islam.

The upright pentagram is considered by many Witches to be the symbol of the Old Religion, and therefore of Witchcraft, and it is often fashioned into an object to wear, such as religious jewelry in the form of pendants, rings, earrings, and bracelets. When the image of the pentagram is an object, it is called a *pentacle*. Another type of pentacle is a ritual, engraved or painted disk, usually made of wood, tile, ceramic, or a metal such as copper, marked with the pentagram and sometimes with other symbols as well. The ritual pentacle is placed at the center of the Witch's altar and is used to represent Elemental Earth and is a place where objects may be set for manifestation or sanctifying during a ritual or spell work. Spell materials or other objects are normally placed on the pentacle for consecration or blessing during rituals. More on this in the section about creating an altar.

Developing a Personal Creed

Utilizing the various concepts of the Old Religion, a Witch may desire to create a personal creed to aid in organizing a coherent understanding of practice. While the Wheel of the Year contains the celebrated eight Sabbats of Witchcraft, a Witch may choose to elaborate on what these holidays mean in relation to the mythology of the chosen deities. The Goddess and the God, represented in the lunar and solar powers honored at the Sabbats and Esbats during the course of the year, have a year-long story beginning and culminating at a particular Sabbat. The Sabbat forming that pivotal point varies according to the perspective of the Practitioner. Some Witches feel the New Year begins at Samhain, others that it begins at the Winter Solstice, so there are options as to how you can draw the elements of the Craft into a coherent sequence. Other sacred days may be added to the individual's calendar according to the mythology of the deities reverenced and the traditional holidays of society.

Because the Divine is seen as immanent, the Spirit resides in all things and in all worlds. This means that part of your creed is a recognition of the unity and kinship of all existence, perhaps observing the Elementals of Earth, Air, Fire, and Water as extensions of the Divine, as related to the Goddess and the God, and personal close kin through the Divine Spirit. Therefore, the creed would include some acknowledgment of the role played by the Elementals in the Witches' spirituality.

Additionally, the ethics of the Craft are also included, and may be expressed as harming none, respecting other Practitioners of the Old Religion as kin, and understanding that the energies sent will return like energy. Overall, you must take care that your actions are not detrimental, selfish, or disrespectful of the independence of others, while at the same time protecting yourself from harm.

A Brief History of Witchcraft

We can have an idea of what the ancient practices of Witchcraft were like from the wall paintings and remains seen in caves occupied in prehistoric times dating from 35,000 through 8000 B.C.E. (Before Current Era). There were rituals for burials that can be detected in modern times, such as placing personal implements with the deceased, and covering the body in red ochre. It is thought by many historians and archaeologists that the red paint is symbolic of the blood of birth, and that since tools, jewelry and other decorative objects, and even food were placed in the graves, there must have been an anticipation of a journey to a new life and possibly a rebirth. Most agree that there was definitely a concept of an afterlife. Altars have also been discovered in these caves, some with the skulls of cave bears with bones thrust through the eye sockets. Figures of pregnant females made in clay or stone show the reverence for the Goddess for fertility and abundance, while cave art of beast master figures indicate either a shamanistic ritual in which the primary animal of the tribe is presented in human form, or that the God is seen as ruling the animals hunted for the continued life of the people, and since there are still ancient religions today in which the God is depicted in this manner, the latter is the more likely antecedent.

There is a strong possibility that the ancient cultures were matrilineal, meaning that descent was traced through the mother rather than through the father as is done in modern times, and that women and men were socially equals or female dominant, depending on the culture and time. Interpreting the evidence and information is a fairly subjective process, which until recent times was biased toward a male-dominant approach that matched the focus of modern mainstream religions. Looking more objectively, however, it becomes clear that there were definite signs of Goddess worship tens of thousands of years ago, but that there were also signs of worship of the God as a Lord of the Animals and the

Wildwood. It may be possible to trace Witchcraft back to the prehistoric period through the archetypal deity images, the observance of the seasons as evidenced by stone circles and celestial notations on surviving prehistoric artifacts, and the conceptualization of the interconnection of the whole of Nature. The actual practices, however, have evolved over time and retain only the sense of the past as is felt by the Practitioner reaching back to connect with the ancestors.

Many laws against Witchcraft have been enacted over the past thousand years attempting to force an end to the Old Religion and acceptance of the New, but while these served to suppress old practices, they did not eradicate them. It was not until the early eighteenth century in England that the legalized torture and execution of those accused of being Witches came to an end. This resulted in the growth and development of a number of magical traditions, mostly grounded in Christianity, Judaism, and Masonic orders as secret societies and occult or spiritualist movements, including the Ancient Order of Druids (1781), the Theosophical Society (1885), and the Hermetic Order of the Golden Dawn (1888). In 1951, the remaining anti-Witchcraft laws were abolished in England. Shortly thereafter, in 1954, Gerald Gardner began writing about Witchcraft, forming what became the Gardnerian Tradition of Witchcraft, and later the word "Wicca" was adopted in an attempt to deflect the negative image of Witchcraft.

Today the term "Traditions" is used to describe the denominations, or varieties, of Witchcraft or Wicca, but is generally used for those denominations dating from the 1940s onward, many of which require a chain of denominational initiations based on the specific Tradition's instruction. Wicca and Witchcraft may be used interchangeably, but there are those who feel that Wicca should refer to the ritual or religious aspects of the Craft and Witchcraft should refer to the magical practices. There are also Witches who feel that the term Wicca refers to specific Traditions with a developing orthodoxy they want no part of, so not all Witches see themselves as Wiccan, and not all Wiccans see themselves as Witches. A person who embraces the Old Religion may decide what name to adopt. Since the energies of Nature, the Elementals, and hence, the Goddess and the God are part of all magical practices, it is basically a matter of semantics. Even the magical aspects involve ritual, although not necessarily one in which there are invocations to the God and the Goddess.

There is also the *Family Tradition* or *Hereditary Witchcraft,* which is derived from those practices of the Old Religion that have been passed along within a family unit or extended family through multiple generations, and whose members may also be called *Bloodline Witches. Natural Witches* are people who feel the energies of Nature and are able to connect with these for the purpose of creating spells and magical crafts. The loving Goddess and God of Nature are the link between all of the Traditions and approaches to Witchcraft, however, no matter what name is given them by individual Witches or covens.

In many places of the world today, Witches are still regarded with distrust, superstition, and fear, mainly because of their ability to commune with Nature and spirits, and because they embrace the knowledge of Nature. Easily blamed by the superstitious for anything that goes wrong in a community, Witches tend to be circumspect about who and what they are, preferring in the main to be Solitary Practitioners and anonymous as they move about in modern society unnoticed. This style of practicing the Craft is called being "in the broom closet" and is one of the main reasons it is so hard to estimate the number of practicing Witches in America and throughout the world today, with estimates varying between several hundred thousand to several million. Whatever the number, the one thing that is certain is that the number is increasing dramatically. Those Witches who are more public about their spirituality are said to be "out of the broom closet," but whether in or out, Solitary or Covened, the matter is one of personal choice.

The actual majority of Witches follow their personal spiritual path alone, practicing the Craft as Solitaries, and thus they are their own Priest or Priestess. They work directly with the energies of Nature and observe the changing seasons, the phases of the Moon, and the special holidays of Witchcraft alone or in the limited company of their immediate family. When Pagan gatherings take place at various times of the year across the country, many Solitary and Coven Witches come together to celebrate their unity in a festive atmosphere marked by camping, outdoor rituals, workshops, drumming, and the fostering of a sense of community. Since there are many different Traditions, a Pagan gathering offers an opportunity for people to exchange ideas within an enjoyable ambiance. Perhaps one of the key elements to Witchcraft is that people accept that there are many paths to the Divine, and as such, the individual Practitioner may follow the path that resonates within, or blaze a new trail altogether.

When a number of Witches living in a region find each other and come together, they may form covens, which are assemblies of practitioners who meet regularly and follow a fairly standardized set of procedures and rituals which they have all agreed upon. While there are fairly consistent practices with all groups of Witches, each group has its own variations to rituals, or identifies with a common envisionment and names for the Goddess and the God. These differences characterize the various Traditions in Witchcraft, and are manners of practice and approaches to the Divine accepted within the coven membership. While the customary number of people, both men and women, in a coven is usually thirteen, including one or two leaders, the numbers actually vary from as few as two to as many as twenty-five to fifty, and the membership may be all female or all male, depending on the Tradition. Having a large coven is highly unusual, simply because the rituals are performed in a Circle, and the larger the group, the larger the space needed for a Circle within which to fit them all. Normally, the ritual Circle is kept to no more than a nine-foot radius, which would fit in a room, since most covens meet at the homes of the members. The coven is led by one or two members, who are called Priest and Priestess or High Priest and High Priestess, depending on the preference of the group. These leaders are often elected by the members, with some covens rotating the position periodically. However, there are also those covens that remain in the hands of the people who formed them, with new covens "hiving" off under former members when the parent coven becomes too large to accommodate everyone in the Circle. For the remainder of this book, however, the focus will be on the practice of the Solitary Witch, and on the basic rituals and magical aspects of Witchcraft.

2

So You Want to Be a Witch?

Deciding to Learn

Perhaps you have decided you want to reclaim your connection with the Earth and release your inner wild child of Nature, but how to begin? There are many ways to approach Witchcraft, and making a change in perspective that is gradual or one that is completely different from a prior lifestyle is a matter of personal decision or necessity. Witchcraft may be practiced within the confines of mainstream religions as folk art, utilizing the prevalent names of the deities, saints, and other holy figures familiar to that religion. Throughout Europe, the folk arts continued in all countries with local variations—this is how some of the practices of the Old Religion were preserved through times of persecution. In much of the Americas, the native population was subjugated and forced to convert to Catholicism, yet they too retained folk traditions by adopting the names of saints for their gods, and in Mexico even finding their own version of Mary with the Virgin of Guadalupe. The site where the vision and miraculous painting of the latter appeared was one held sacred to a local Earth Goddess. To the priesthood, accepting the native image of

Mary was convenient to Catholic conversion. North American tribes were more often converted by force to a Protestant version of Christianity, with efforts made to eradicate all Native American spiritual practices, creating a lasting resentment by the persecution of those who did not conform to the new religion. Only in the past century have Native Americans in the Northern Hemisphere been successful in reclaiming their religious heritage.

African slaves brought to the Americas were also forced to convert from their aboriginal religions to embrace Christianity, and they responded to this challenge by adopting the images of Jesus, Mary, and the various saints to represent their own deities. By using the names accepted by society, the attributes of the old deities were merely shifted until such time as it became possible to return to the old names. Today, Santería, Candomblé, and Macumba have mostly reclaimed the names of the deities and images of African heritage. The same can be said for those Witches of European heritage who have quietly practiced their Craft using the names of saints for the Gods and Goddesses, and celebrated the traditional holidays under the culturally accepted names, while understanding the Pagan origins of these special days. Thus, folk art Witches may invoke the Power as the energies of socially accepted deities, angels, saints, and spirits, while adapting earlier cultural images into their practice.

Many Pagan practices were adopted by the Catholic Church under Pope Gregory the Great, in the seventh century C.E., as a method for bringing acceptance of the new religion to Europe's Pagan population and thus extending the power of the Church over an ever-increasing amount of territory. The holy days of the Old Religion were made into those of the saints and incorporated into the mythology of the new religion. The myths of Dionysos, Cybele and Attis, Mithras, and other very popular religions at the dawn of Christianity were drawn into the new religion. The Pagan holy days of the Winter Solstice (Yule), the Spring Equinox

(Ostara), and Lughnassadh became Christmas (although scholars argue that Jesus had to have been born in June), Easter (although this word is the Saxon name of the Goddess of Spring), and Assumption Day (although there are different religious traditions as to whether Virgin Mary died or was bodily taken up into Heaven). The Pagan sacred sites had their temples destroyed and churches built over them; the rituals of the Mass came directly from the rituals of meeting the Roman emperor as established by Diocletian; and the customs of lighting candles at shrines, laying flowers at natural wells, using incense and images of the different aspects of the Divine were all adopted, with the Holy Family and the saints taking the place of the ancient deities. Thus, because there has been so much interweaving of the old with the new, it is not difficult to practice the ancient ways within a culturally acceptable and modern societal context.

Witchcraft is also practiced as personal magics, bringing the individual into union with the Universe and enhancing personal energy with that of herbs and other natural objects. In this style, there is no reference to any deity, but rather the Divine is approached as distilled through those objects used in spell work to purposefully move energy for achieving a goal. Ritual, magical tools, and conscious spellwork are actually functioning through the Divine emanations known as the Elementals. This is when the Witch begins to categorize spell-casting correlations and attributes called *lists of correspondences,* placing these in a journal called a *Book of Shadows* for consistency in magic work. Religion is very muted in this approach, save as the Witch and the unnamed All work together through the powers of Nature, using trust in instinct and intuition as the main guide for magic. Ethics is still needed here because the idea of balance permeates the magical practice, be it in the form of giving a gift to receive a gift, knowing that energy sent returns equally or threefold, or understanding karmic destiny as determined by one's actions.

Witchcraft is also a religion in its own right, and the magics of the Craft are worked in a partnership between the Goddess and the God and the Witch. Besides the lists of correspondences in the Book of Shadows, there are also rituals for celebrating the phases of the Moon and the eight Sabbats which are the spokes to the Wheel of the Year. For the Solitary Practitioner, a Self-Initiation may be done for introduction and for seeking arcane wisdom, and later a further Dedication may be approached for a complete union with the Divine. Many Wiccan Traditions have three degrees of initiation, with the *first degree* being the introduction, during which time the new Witch learns about the Craft; the *second degree* being an elevation to High Priest or High Priestess allowing the more experienced Witch to initiate others; and the *third degree* being a recognition that the Witch is sufficiently experienced to form her or his own coven. But for practical purposes, the ideas behind these degrees are incorporated in the Solitary practice of Self-Initiation, followed by study and practice for a year and a day, and a periodic Re-Affirmation thereafter. A Self-Dedication may be performed by personal ritual later on, or it may occur as the experiencing of a spontaneous opening of the lines of communication between the Witch and the Divine. The only difference between the advancement of the individual through experience and that of the degree system is the ritual according to the tradition of the coven. The Solitary acts are between the Witch and the Divine—hence, the Goddess and the God are invoked by the Witch through the Self-Initiation for introduction and learning, the commitment is usually reaffirmed at least once a year, and there may finally be a complete union between Witch and the Divine in a Self-Dedication. Not all Witches pass through these stages of growth in the form of rituals, but instead may note a difference in their perceptions and attitudes as they live the Craft. As a religion, the magic of Witchcraft is often directed through personal communion with the God and the

Goddess, but the Divine energy may be indirectly channeled through the Witch by working with the Elementals and the objects of Nature such as herbs and crystals. Additionally, the Solitary Witch also observes the Sabbats and the Esbats, either through rituals or through recognition of the time and with activities associated with these times.

The most important step in becoming a Witch is making that first statement, which is the heart of the Self-Initiation. This is how a person states his or her desire to learn about the Craft, to become a Witch. The desire comes from the heart, and the ritual act is actually a demonstration of what has already taken place internally. To get to that point, the would-be Witch will have come to a world-view with a Divine that is Goddess and God; an understanding that life is meant to be enjoyed; and a comprehension that the individual is part of the living Earth that needs to be revered. Not only does this person recognize the connection with all things, but with the Elementals, who are emanations of the Divine and part of the person, in physical form and strengths (Earth), in breath and thought (Air), in ambitions and energy (Fire), and in blood, water, and emotions (Water). This feeling of union is also a comprehension of the flow of energy through the Self and Nature, the Universe, and the Divine; thus magic may be worked simply by gathering, directing, and sending that energy to accomplish a task before returning it to Nature. For many Witches and other magical practitioners in other Pagan systems, this unifying and sacred energy is simply called *the Power*. The Power can be accessed through meditation—a quiet time in which the Witch focuses the mind to receive information rather than attempting to direct or shape it. An ethical standard may have already evolved naturally in the supplicant since the awareness of interconnection will stimulate the need for compassion and care in actions and thoughts. This standard may be put in writing, or the adoption of the basic Witches' Rede in chapter 1 will help in defining Craft ethics, and should be recited at the Sabbat and Esbat observances or rituals.

Names in Witchcraft

If you have decided that you want to explore the path of Witchcraft, you can begin with a Self-Initiation, announcing yourself to the Goddess and the God, and asking for their help in your education. It is a good idea to prepare in advance for this simple ritual, and one of the things you should already decide upon is a Working Name. This is different from your birth name or legal name, being one that you have chosen and which you will use whenever performing magic. Most religions have some way of distinguishing the moment of transformation from nonparticipant to membership. In the Catholic Church, the taking of a saint's name is part of the Confirmation ceremony. In many Protestant Churches, a similar event occurs or the person receives a new title such as Brother, Sister, or Saint to designate the new membership status. With Witchcraft, the Working Name is chosen and carried in secret as a bond between the Witch and the Divine. If the Witch works magic or conducts rituals with other Witches, a second name is used in front of these people, and it is called the Craft Name. With your Self-Initiation, you are creating a special covenant between yourself and the Goddess and the God.

Later on, when you have more experience and have decided that you have found the spiritual path that speaks to your heart, you may want to do a Dedication ritual. At this time, the Goddess and the God will give you a new and secret Working Name, and you can use the old one that you created as your Craft Name or discard it. This new name from the Dedication is one that defines you, and is never revealed to anyone, for it is a sacred trust between you and the Goddess and the God. They may reveal to you

Their secret names, or if not, you may ask Them and They will answer. For now, the Initiation is first, and you will not be doing a Dedication until much later.

Working Names are normally derived from something the person enjoys, finds attractive, or is otherwise drawn to in Nature. Some people adopt a deity name, but more likely the name will be based on a personal appreciation for something in Nature such as animals, trees, flowers, herbs, minerals, and weather. Some typical examples of Working Names would be Willowleaf, Elderflower, Tourmaline, Amber, Bear, Moth, Traveler, Explorer, Mist, Rainfall, Autumn, Summer, Luna, AstroNightSky, Waterfall, Timber, and Mossyrock. So you are thinking about something in Nature that appeals to you, concepts that relate to you in particular based on your hobbies or line of work, and you may even draw together several ideas into one name. The main point is that it is a name that has meaning to you. You could also draw your name from astrological events and things from the universe, utilizing stars, solar flares, comets, nebulas, and so forth as a portion of your name. Or you could simply use a regular name that has always appealed to you, and by investigating the derivation, find a meaningful connection. In this way, a name such as Isadora can be seen as derived from one who follows the Goddess Isis. There are any number of ways to pick a personal Working Name, and all that matters is that you are satisfied with it and that it is different from your birth name.

When you take on the Working Name, you are alerting your subconscious mind that something different is about to occur—it takes you out of the ordinary world frame and prepares you to enter into the magical realm. This aids in getting you into an altered state of mind wherein you will be more able to move energy and commune with the Goddess and the God. You will use this name for spell castings and for the rituals familiar to Witchcraft— the Esbats and the Sabbats.

In general, the Craft Name is one you choose to call yourself by and introduce yourself to others in the Craft. A Craft Name may be used openly and when visiting a coven or working with other Witches, and is sometimes called an *outer court* name. The Working Name is a secret one that you choose to go by when working magic and ritual in private. After doing a Dedication Ritual, the Goddess and the God will bestow a new Working Name, one that defines you, and is also kept secret. The Working Name is *never* revealed to anyone, not even family and friends. If someone learns your Working Name, you will need to release it and choose another. For Witches who are part of a coven, there is also the Eke Name, or Coven Name, which is either chosen by the person being initiated into the coven, or is bestowed on the person by the coven leaders, usually by the High Priestess. This name is used *only* in the coven environment and is called an *inner court* name.

The Moons of the Witch: The Esbats

The Esbats are rituals of the Full Moon and the New (Dark) Moons—times to receive learning from the Goddess. The Lady is mostly honored during the lunar phases of the Full Moon and New Moon (at the last waning crescent), when magical workings are usually done. While the Dark Moon (fully obscured) may also be celebrated, this phase is best for meditational work rather than active spell casting. The Esbats are times for drawing in the Goddess energies, either for spell work or for personal understanding and communication. Divinations and meditations may be done as desired, for while there may be a ritual framework, the individual practitioner has the freedom to do as needed. This freedom to play around with the structure of the rituals and to incorporate what you want into the Esbat is probably one of the more difficult things for the new Witch to learn. Often we are accustomed to being told what to do and how to do it, but Witchcraft turns this responsibility over to the Witch. You are in charge of your rituals and your development, and you learn through asking the Goddess for her assistance in your training.

The Full Moon honors the Goddess as Great Mother and recognizes her influence in the tides of the Earth and in our lives. There are normally twelve Full Moons in a solar year, but sometimes there are thirteen, meaning that one solar month will embrace two Full Moons. This second Full Moon is the Blue Moon, and it is in this one that spiritual energy is enhanced. When there are two Dark Moons in the same solar month, the second one will be enhanced by psychic energy and is called the Sidhe Moon. The reason I specify *solar* month is because there are also *lunar* months, which will not match the more familiar calendar. The lunar month is measured by the cycle of the Moon, while the solar months are the calendar ones with thirty or thirty-one days, except for February which usually has twenty-eight days, unless it is a leap year when it has twenty-nine days.

The Full Moons follow the calendar months beginning with the one in December, with a Blue Moon being a random event in whatever month it happens to fall. When a second Full Moon occurs, it can be in any season. There are different names associated with the Moons, but these are common ones: December: *Oak Moon*; January: *Wolf Moon*; February: *Storm Moon*; March: *Sap Moon*; April: *Seed Moon*; May: *Hare Moon*; June: *Dryad Moon*; July: *Herb Moon*; August: *Barleycorn* (or *Corn*) *Moon*; September: *Harvest Moon*; October: *Hunter's Moon*; November: *Snow Moon*.

The Seasons of the Witch: The Sabbats

The Witches' year is depicted like a wheel with eight spokes. The spokes indicate the celebrated Sabbats, and these are composed of four solar festivals called the Lesser Sabbats or the Quarters, and four agricultural festivals called the Greater Sabbats or the Cross-Quarters. There are many ancient standing stone circles in Europe where the Quarters of the year are marked by specially positioned stones that catch the first rays of sunlight on the summer and winter solstices and on the spring and fall (autumn) equinoxes. Some people believe that such sites as Stonehenge in England were prehistoric calendars used for agricultural and religious purposes, but no one knows exactly what rituals or ceremonies were originally conducted there. In Witchcraft, these Quarters and Cross-Quarters form the eight major festivals of the year, revolving around the mythology of the God and the Goddess. While there are variations on the story about the yearly passage of the God through these special times, the archetypes are fairly consistent and the differences are not all that relevant.

Because the Divine is One and manifest in all things, the aspects of the Divine may interchange roles. Either the Lady or the Lord may represent the Sun, Moon, Grain, Harvest, Waters of Life, Universe, Sky, Earth, Life, Death, Passage, Resurrection in Body and/or in Spirit. The Lady and the Lord symbolize female and male fertility. They are both Power and Passage, honored with rites of burning lamps, candles, and torches; with salt and water, bread and wine, and flowers and grain. They both represent the passing of the seasons through solstices and equinoxes as well as the cycle of agriculture from seed preparation through planting, tending, and harvesting. The correlation of the cycles of Sun phases and agriculture is made with the life cycle, depicting a person's transition through the stages of life from pregnancy, to birth, youth, maturation and parenthood, old age, death passage, and rebirth. Thus the Lord yearly shows us through his passage in the solar cycles how our own lives transit through our own years. He is the Sun, and the Lady is the Earth, culminating with the energy of the Sun entering the life-supporting grains of the Earth, and giving the spirit of life into the fruits of the vines that refresh us. Through the Sabbats, the interaction is between the God and the Goddess, with the Earth, Nature, and ourselves benefiting from their yearly ritual of passage through the turnings of the Wheel of the Year, showing that the cycle is never-ending, and demonstrating the immortality of the spirit.

The Lesser Sabbats, or Quarters, are also called the Green Sabbats or the Seasonal Sabbats. These are: *Yule* (the Winter Solstice) on December 21; *Ostara* (the Spring Equinox) on March 21; *Litha* (the Summer Solstice) on June 21; and *Mabon* (the Autumn Equinox and second harvest of vine and fruit) on September 21. The Seasonal Sabbats have remained as part of modern mainstream culture simply because they do mark the changing of the seasons on the calendar. The Greater Sabbats, or Cross-Quarters, are also called the White Sabbats or the Fire Sabbats. These are: *Samhain* on October 31, the third or gourd harvest; *Imbolc* on February 2, the preparation for planting; *Beltane* on May 1, planting; and *Lughnassadh* on August 1, the first or bread harvest. In olden times, great bonfires were lit on hilltops during the Fire Sabbats for the community to celebrate around and run their cattle through the smoky embers to kill parasites and protect them from harmful influences. Today, the fires are more likely to be small and as individualized as a campfire, fireplace fire, or a votive candle in a cauldron.

Traditions have different ways of looking at the Sabbats. Some Witches divide the year in half, with the God ruling the Dark Months of the Autumn and Winter seasons, and the Goddess ruling the Light Months of the Spring and Summer seasons, but others see the interaction of the Goddess and the God throughout the year, with only their individual aspects changing with the seasons. The God is called the Oak King during the waxing solar year from Yule to Litha, and the Holly King during the waning solar year from Litha to Yule. He is both Sun God and Lord of Shadows; Hunter and Greenman; Horned God of the Wildwood and

Animals, and Jack of the Green; the one who collects the spirits who seek passage through the Goddess into new life, and the one who gives them repose in Underworld. The Lady is the One Who Transforms, the Changer. It is through her that the Lord begets himself in her, dies, passes to Underworld, then is reborn of her. She changes, but is never-ending, and she is both Crone and Mother at the same time; thus her Tomb is also the Womb. It is through her that the spirit travels from death into new life, through her Cauldron of Rebirth. Overlapping ancient customs and practices have been merged together in the Wheel of the Year, and you are able to pick out those themes that have meaning for you without fear of losing something of the whole—somehow it all comes together with blurred edges and blended seams.

Attuning to the God and the Goddess changes one forever— sparks new hope for the individual and for the planet. Both the Dark Aspects of the God and the Goddess—Lord of Shadows and Crone—the Bright Aspects—Horned God and Maiden/ Mother are accepted as part of the Balance of Nature. The Divine is both Creation and Destruction; Abundant Nature and Destructive Nature; Order and Chaos; Matter and Energy. Since all life is joined in the Dual Deity, the Two Who Are One, and to each other, the spirit cannot be destroyed, only changed or dipped in and out of the Lady's cauldron of life. The religion then is the worship or reverence of the Life Force represented in the Dual Deity as a Conscious Unity or Sacred Spirit shared by all life. This reverence is expressed through the activities, ceremonies, and rituals of the Sabbats, dedicated to cycles of fertility, of planting and harvest, of solar and lunar phases, and of the mythology of the God and Goddess.

The Wheel of the Year

The year begins at Samhain for many Traditions, while others begin with Yule, Imbolc, Ostara, or even Hogmanay Eve, familiar as New Year's Eve. Using this latter cultural calendar event, we can look at it as the time when the passage of the Crone is honored, for now Winter is in full bloom of cold and snow, and She carries the Newborn King in Her arms. At Imbolc, the God is brought to His Mother, and begins to grow older as She grows younger. He becomes Her companion in Ostara to awaken the Earth, and then Her lover at Beltane. At Litha, the mature God impregnates Her with Himself, and passes His essence as Oak King into the care of the Goddess while He now becomes the Holly King, older and wiser. When They wed at Lughnassadh, He freely gives His life essence into the Earth, fully aware that He now will lead the transition of death passage in Samhain through the tomb of the Crone into the womb of the Mother. At Yule, the transition is completed with the birth of the Oak King, who takes rulership of the Turning of the Wheel, so that the Holly King aspect now departs, leaving presents for children as for His newborn self. The sleigh He rides is the boat of the dying year, the eight reindeer are the Sabbats, and He heads North to the realm of the Crone. There this aspect abides until ready to replace the Oak King again at Litha, and so the Wheel turns ever onward, with the seasons following in their proper course. The image of the Holly King is the same one as the Lord of Shadows, Santa Claus, and Old Father Time, and the Oak King is the same as the Infant Sun King, Baby Jesus, and the New Year's Baby.

As you can see, there are several different themes in the mythology. This is due to a combining of the religions of agrarian, herding, and hunting societies into the modern revival of the Old Religion. You can take those themes that appeal to you and discard those that do not, but it is good to know what some of the ideas are so that when you come into contact with other Witches and Pagans, you will understand their perspective. Here is an easy guide for the Sabbats, with their approximate dates and in order, with some of the meanings embodied by them:

Yule — Winter Solstice, December 21

1. The Oak King aspect of the God is born of the Mother Goddess

2. The Holly King aspect of the God departs to the North (or to the Underworld), leaving presents for children in honor of the Oak King

3. The Goddess is the Mother of the Sun God/Oak King

4. The Goddess is also the Crone of Winter

Imbolc — Purification and Cleansing Fire, February 1

1. The Mother aspect of the Goddess is cleansed and purified; The Crone aspect takes the infant God to herself as Mother

2. Milk flows for lambs and for the baby God (the infant Sun or Oak King)

3. Quickening of the Earth and readying of the seeds for planting

4. The Goddess is changing from her Mother aspect to her Maiden aspect

Ostara — Spring Equinox, March 21

1. The Maiden aspect of the Goddess brings Spring to the land

2. The Youthful Oak King (or Greenman) aspect of the God walks the land with the Maiden aspect of the Goddess, awakening the Earth together

3. The Crone aspect of the Goddess has departed to Underworld or to the North (if the weather turns cold again, you

could say that the Crone has returned momentarily because
she forgot her boots)

Beltane — Fertility and Enlivening Fire, May 1

1. The youthful Oak King (or Greenman) aspect of the God
   unites in love with the Maiden aspect of the Goddess

2. May Day flowers, maypole dancing, and bonfires to encourage fertility

3. Communion with the Faerie Realms for good fortune and
   blessings

Litha — Summer Solstice, June 21

1. The God changes from Youthful Oak King to Holly King Sage

2. The Holly King impregnates the Goddess with his Oak King
   aspect

3. Some Traditions see this as the Marriage of the God and the
   Goddess

4. Some Traditions see the Holly King slaying the Oak King,
   with the reverse happening at Yule (in this view, they are
   called the Tanist Twins, meaning that they are heirs to one
   another as the Celtic chiefs used to designate their heirs early
   in their rulership)

5. Midsummer celebration of communion with the Faerie
   Realms for good relationships

Lughnassadh — Bread Harvest and
Solar Sacrifice Fire, August 1

1. The Sun aspect of the God enters the Mother Earth aspect
   of the Goddess in Marriage, giving his energy into the grain,
   which is now considered his body

2. First Harvest/Bread Harvest—grains

Mabon — Autumn Equinox, September 21

1. The God in the Earth now gives his spirit into the vines (apples/barleycorn), and wine (cider/whiskey) is now considered his blood

2. The God rules in Underworld as Lord of Shadows;

3. The Goddess is alone, becoming the Crone, but also Mother-to-Be since she is pregnant with the Oak King aspect of the God

4. Second Harvest/Vine and Fruit

Samhain — Death and Rebirth Fire, October 31

1. The Crone Goddess enters Underworld to rule beside the God in his Lord of Shadows aspect

2. The God also travels the skies as the Horned Hunter, wearing antlers and leading a group of spirits called the Wild Hunt or the Rade

3. Veil between the worlds is thinnest, allowing spirits to commune with the living when the God passes into the Crone Goddess, to be reborn at Yule, making Her both the tomb and the womb

4. Third Harvest/Gourds, Squash, and Beans

The Circle: Casting and Opening

When casting spells and doing the rituals of Esbats and Sabbats, a Circle is used to provide you with a purified spherical space wherein you can stand between the worlds, raise and direct energy, and commune with the Divine. It is called a *sacred space*, and provides you with a way of taking yourself out of the ordinary frame of mind and into a special awareness for magical workings. Spells and rituals may certainly be done without casting a Circle, but for the beginning Witch, the casting of a Circle makes an especially effective imprint on the distinctiveness of the activities taking place, offering a womb-like security. Some people say the Circle is cast for protection, and this is true in the sense that you are more vulnerable to extraneous energies while focused on energy work.

By creating the Circle, you create a buffer between your work area—a temporary temple as it were—and the rest of the world. The Circle is cast as an enveloping space that not only goes around you, but is above and below you, cutting through ceilings, floors, furniture, and walls if need be. It is like being inside a bubble or an egg, within which you raise and fashion magical energy to birth into manifestation that which you seek to accomplish. When the ritual or spell casting is finished, the Circle is opened, with the Circle's energy returning into you.

Because you are dealing with energy, you must be sure to always *ground and center* before casting your Circle, and to return the excess energy into the Earth when you open your Circle. You ground and center prior to any magical work, so as part of the process of casting a Circle, you will have already done this and will be ready for the ritual, meditation, divination, or spell work being conducted within the Circle. The reason for grounding and centering before all magical work is to avoid depleting your personal energy levels. You are augmenting your own energy with that of the Earth. Begin by being still, gathering within and pushing out through your feet (and palms if need be) into the ground all the static, chaotic internal energies within you. Now feel the inner calmness, centered around the heart, and draw up through your feet the strong Earth energy, visualizing it coming up even through the floor if you are indoors, feeling the power and energy rising up and intertwining with your own energies up through the legs, body, arms, neck, and head, out the top of the head, circled around, and up again until all portions of the body are in balance. Once this power is felt and is in balance, then you are ready to cast the Circle and begin your magical work.

To visualize the flow of energy, try thinking of the Earth as having a vast reservoir of energy that you can tap into at will. It is rather like pretending you are a tree and there is a taproot extending from your feet into the rich Earth. It does not matter if you are standing on the ground or on the fifteenth floor of an apartment building. You visualize that your taproot extends through the floors, the foundation, the street, and into the rich Earth beneath. Plunge the taproot deep into the ground where you now connect with the Earth. The taproot is Nature's straw for trees, and you draw up to drink in the abundant energy. Like the tree, you bring the energy up into your body, and cycle it through your whole body. But now you are also bringing all the energies into balance, spreading it equally throughout your body. As you work magic or do divinations, you can draw up more sustaining energy whenever you start to feel a little drained. Just replenish the energy supply as you work your magics.

Once the work is completed, and you have released the raised energy into your magical endeavor, you need to touch the ground or floor with the palms of your hands to let the excess energy drain out. Now you open the Circle, and as you complete this act, you are again bringing the energy back inside yourself, and again, you balance your personal energies, keeping what you need and returning the remainder to the Earth by touching the ground or floor again with your palms. The palms of the hands and the soles of the feet are terrific energy conductors, as is the top of your head.

By grounding when the magical work is completed and the Circle is opened, you avoid overloading your personal energy levels. By touching the Earth or floor with your palms after magical work, you feel the excess energy drain out, leaving you with a balance of personal energy, augmented only by that amount of Earth necessary for healthy functioning of the body. Too much retained energy will result in headache, depression, or irritability. Too little will result in fatigue, depression, or faintness. You must find the inner balance, and adjust according to how you feel. Remember that you can fine tune the energy at any time. If you have finished your magical work and realize you are feeling irritable, just release a little more energy into the ground through your palms or feet. If you are suddenly tired, draw up some more energy through your feet and cycle it through your body. There are a number of different ways to cast and open the Circle, but there is a fairly standard method. Once you understand the basics, you can always make any ritual as elaborate or as simple as you like. The components of rituals are fairly consistent. These are tried and true methods found to work through the years by experienced Witches. While you may take shortcuts, know that the results will be much more satisfying if you follow the procedures others have learned over time.

Setting Up Your First Altar

It is always best to plan your activities in advance and have everything set up and ready for when you begin. You will need a table or other type of surface to act as your altar, where the materials of your magical work will be placed and that will act as the center of focus for your activities. The area can be the top of a dresser or chest of drawers, a desk, a table, or even a box. Put a cloth over it to make it a special area—a print sarong or scarf makes a fine altar cloth, or you can use a tablecloth you reserve for magical works. Some people like to make their own altar cloths, incorporating a design or pentagram at the center of the cloth. The altar is divided into three sections, with the left side being the Goddess area, the right side being the God area, and the center section belonging to both the Goddess and the God, showing them as in Balance. The altar should be placed so that when you are facing it, you are facing North or East, depending on your preference.

North represents the realm of wisdom and magical power, while the East represents the realm of intuition, opening awareness, and the power of the Sun. The North may represent the region of a Goddess of Witches (Hecate, Isis, Diana), while the East may represent the region of a Sun God (Lugh, Ra, Apollo).

There are certain tools that are considered to have Goddess energy and those that have God energy, and these are laid on the appropriate side of the altar, with the center section being the area where the action takes place. The tools can be bought, handmade, or picked up from Nature, and thus they can range from fairly expensive to absolutely free. The basic tools are the wand, the knife, called the athame (*ah-tham'mee*), and the cauldron—but a well-equipped altar will also have a pentacle, a chalice or cup for beverage, a bell, incense and holder, three candles and holders, a bowl for salt and a bowl for water, and possibly statues or other deity images such as a shell for the Goddess and antlers/bull's horn for the God. While not necessary to an altar, the images do add a nice touch. The candles may be in separate holders or one candelabra. For Esbats, the colors of the three candles are generally blue on the left for the Goddess, orange on the right for the God, and white or yellow in the center for Both in Balance. Besides these tools, you will also place on the altar the ingredients for your spell work, and your Book of Shadows or journal with your ritual and spell written out for you to follow.

On the next page is an example of how an altar may be set up. You will note that food and a libation bowl are included in this example. That is because you may want to include a ritual called "Cakes and Wine" after you have conducted spell work and before you open the Circle. This is a way of honoring the Divine and also to return to normal awareness. This ritual is used primarily in Esbats and Sabbats, but is often included for after the spell casting has been completed.

Altar Layout

Candelabra or three separate candles

Goddess
[symbol/image]

Both
[symbol/image]

God
[symbol/image]

Chalice

Bell

Incense

Water Bowl

Pentacle

Salt Bowl

Wand

Cauldron

Athame/Bolline

Supplies
(Oils, Herbs)

Libation Bowl

Food & Supplies
(Matches, Incense)

Book of Shadows
(Work Materials)

The pentacle is a solid item, usually of wood, ceramic tile, or metal and it sits at the center of the altar to represent the Elemental Earth. During spell work, items may be set on top of the pentacle for consecrating and manifestation, and the cauldron is often placed on top of it during spell work. A paper pentacle may be used if you do not have a more substantial one; just be careful that the materials you place on it will not burn it. Today there are lots of catalogs and stores that sell the kinds of tools used by Witches, but you can always make your own tools.

The Book of Shadows

The Book of Shadows is the essential tool of the Witch. While it is usually handwritten in a journal or loose-leaf good quality vellum or parchment, it can also be typed into the personal computer and printed out utilizing as plain or as fancy a font as desired. This item contains the procedures for casting the Circle, the rituals for the Esbats and Sabbats, the correlations of magical properties of such things as herbs, stones, colors, days of the week and hours of the day, and the spells and any other information the Witch wants to keep handy for easy reference. This is the Witch's cookbook, diary, and book of ritual, through which magical practice is refined and made consistent. Indeed, much of the information in this book may be transcribed into your personal Book of Shadows. The book will grow as your practice grows, and cover the areas of magic that appeal to you. Some Witches like to focus on divination, others on working with stones and crystals, so their books will reflect their personal tastes.

Components of Magical Ritual

The first thing to do when preparing for magical work is to purify yourself. This is done with a quiet ritual bath, usually including sea salt or rock salt in the bath water, and possibly some herbs in a tea ball or muslin bag through which the water will be able to flow. Herbs may be used individually or as a combination of such herbs as rosemary, thyme, marjoram, lavender, rose petals, calendula, hops, or burdock root for cleansing and purification prior to ritual. It is very helpful to burn some incense and light a candle for the bath area, and while in the bath, you are able to consciously ground and center, letting all the tensions and mundane annoyances slip away into the water as you relax and focus on the magical experience awaiting you. When you rise and let out the water, see these extraneous energies as going down the drain. The same thing applies if you are using a shower. Let the water soothe you and carry away all the chaotic and stressful energies, leaving you feeling relaxed.

Now you are ready to put on a ritual robe. Some Witches like to work skyclad, meaning in the nude, but most prefer to wear some special clothes reserved for magical workings. This adds to the sense of doing something out of the ordinary, of embarking upon some special time and enterprise. Robes are usually loose and comfortable, generally made of cotton or muslin, but could also be of silk or velvet. The colors play an important part for the focus of your work. Here are some suggestions for meanings ascribed to robe or dress colors: *oranges and reds*—for vitality, energy, and for the Sabbats; *white and creamy* muslin—for purification and for the Esbats; *black*—for protection, truth, and warding negativity; *greens*—for Nature, the Wildwood, the Lady and the Lord of Nature, herbs, the Earth, and the Other People (Elves, Fairies, Dryads, Devas, etc.); *gray and pale lavender*—for Otherworld or Faerie, and for the Sidhe (Elves); *purples*—for spiritual awareness and intuition; *blues*—for water and sky, and for psychic awareness; *yellows*—for divination, solar energy, and psychic powers; and *browns* for grounding and animal magics. Most Witches end up with a couple of different robes and wear what is appropriate to the season and the purpose of the ritual.

Now that you are bathed and robed, you purify the space in which you will conduct the magical event. You sweep the area *deosil* (clockwise) with a special broom, called a *besom* (bess'um), which is used only for magical work. You may want to now light candles at the Quarters, also moving deosil around the Circle. One neat idea is to get four small wall shelves to hang up around a room where you do your magics. On each shelf place a votive candle in a fireproof container, and as you begin casting your Circle, you can light the candles, using a different color for each of the Elementals: green for Earth at the North; yellow for Air at the East; red for Fire at the South; and blue for Water at the West. Otherwise, you may want to designate the Quarters with something that symbolizes them to you, such as a rock at the North, a feather at the East, a piece of pumice, obsidian, or lava at the South, and a shell at the West. These are merely suggestions—you could use all stones, perhaps in different colors, or marked with the Elemental designs: $\triangledown$ for Earth; $\triangle$ for Air; $\triangle$ for Fire; $\triangledown$ for Water.

Next comes the casting of the Circle in which you visualize a blue-white light coming from the wand or the hand you favor as you walk deosil around the Circle again. You will asperge the Circle with blessed water, cense it with incense, call the Elementals, and welcome the Goddess and the God, then conduct the ritual or observance for which the Circle was cast. During this latter event you will be raising energy and directing it for consecrations or spell work, then you ground the residual energy. The Cakes and Wine ritual helps to bring the magical event to a close, after which you will farewell the Divine and the Elementals, open the Circle, and make any final benediction you may desire. In the next chapter, we will look at Circle casting and opening, a Self-Initiation Ritual, and the rituals for the Esbats and Sabbats.

3

Getting Started

Basic Tools

In the last chapter there was a layout for an altar and some of the tools used by Witches were introduced. When collecting or buying your tools, you can prepare in advance by asking the Elementals or the Lady and the Lord to bring you into contact with the tool you desire, at a price you can afford. You do this just by talking to them—although anyone who sees you would think you are talking to thin air, so do this either in private or discreetly. A good time to ask the Elementals for something is when there is a breeze blowing or a windy day—it sends your request out quickly.

Be sure to state the amount you are willing to pay for an item, and envision the item as you want it to appear. By picturing the tool in your mind, you let the Elementals see it as well, especially Elemental Air, which carries thoughts and enhances intellect. When you then encounter the item, buy it so you do not offend the Elementals who brought it to you by your own request. Here is an important point: *do not ask for things you do not want or do not intend to buy*. Another important point with magical tools is to *avoid haggling over the price*. That is why you tell the Elementals how much you are willing to pay—which may be less than how much you can afford. So when actively seeking magical tools, ask for what you want and state at what price you want it. It could be that you want simply to find the item in Nature, and this is where Elemental Earth will be a big help.

As with all things in Witchcraft, the balance of equal returns applies, so before you take something in Nature (such as a thin branch from a tree for a wand), you have to give something. This can be water, milk, grain, a coin, a blessing, or something of that sort. The energy sent out in the giving of a gift opens the way for you to receive the energy of the gift given to you by the object in Nature, such as a tree letting you cut off a piece for your wand. Whether you buy a tool or take one from Nature, you are binding it to you through the exchange of money or through the gifting process—this helps make it *your* tool. Because tools are bound to a person, it is considered highly offensive in Witchcraft to touch or handle someone else's magical tools or jewelry. This is a breach of trust, and means that the person will have to reconsecrate the item. You may ask permission to do so, for some items are not perceived by individual Witches as sacrosanct as others, but never do so without first being given permission. You also endanger yourself, because you engage in an exchange of energy, and this may not be at all what you want.

Athame

By looking at these tools in more detail, you can see how they differ and how they are used. The athame is a ritual knife used to direct magical energy; this is usually a black-handled, two-edged knife, meaning the blade is sharp on both sides, but it may be dull rather than sharp as this is not a cutting tool. This is one of the primary ritual tools, and may be made of wood, stone, horn, metal, or jet, and may even be a regular paring knife if visualized as the ritual tool. The tools of the *Kitchen Witch* are taken from those used in daily work around the house, being considered as charged by the energy of the user, yet visualized in a magical activity as further empowered. An athame may also be a letter opener or pocket knife, just so long as it is seen as a ritual tool. This means that you can have an athame that other people will not recognize as anything out of the ordinary, but that you will know has special uses. The color of the handle may vary, but black is traditional.

Wand

The other most typical tool associated with the Witch is the wand. This tool should be about twelve to sixteen inches long, measuring from fingertips to the bend of your arm, or elbow. It can be taken from a tree once you have asked the tree for permission to use it, and have given the tree a gift—examples of this have already been suggested above. You select the wood of your wand, and you can also buy or make one of metal or glass, sometimes with crystals at either end. But the traditional wand is of a wood such as oak, willow, hazel, apple, or elder. Each of these woods is considered to possess certain influences, and you select or purchase your wand according to the influence on which you want to focus. Some Witches have more than one wand, using different ones for different types of magic or ritual, and some wands are tipped with a crystal, a nut, or a pine cone. The wand may look like an ordinary stick, about ¼- to ½-inch thick, or be a rod or tube of a metal such as copper or silver, or glass such as lead crystal. It can be solid or hollowed out and stuffed with small crystals and herbs as desired. When putting things inside a hollow wand, look at the list of correspondences found later in the book for ideas of which herbs and stones to use to suit your purposes. The important thing, however, is that the tool appeals to you and you are drawn to it. The woods most frequently used as wands are of oak, willow, and hazel, but here is a listing of some of the basic influences associated with various types of wood:

Alder: water magic, strength; apple: love, beauty, spring, Goddess energy

Ash: studies, health, intensify magic, God energy

Aspen: open intuitive powers, Otherworld communication

Birch: purifying, vitality, beginnings, Goddess energy

Elder: cleansing, Fairies, changes, evolution, Goddess energy

Fir/Pine: prosperity, power, discretion, objectivity

Hazel: Witchcraft skills, wisdom, creativity, enhance perceptiveness, Goddess energy

Rowan (mountain ash): protection, enhance magic, insightfulness, cleansing, Goddess energy

Oak: power, balance, protection, success, truth, fertility, God energy

Willow: psychic power, lunar magics, intuition, spirits, Goddess energy

Cauldron

Another tool typical of the Witch is the cauldron. This is a metal pot with three feet that keep the bottom from touching a surface. The cauldron is used for magical work. Although you can use something of a different material such as ceramic or pottery, metal provides the greatest safety. The pot should be large enough so you can burn things in it without causing a fire hazard. If you cannot get one with a lid, keep at hand a lid from some other pan or something solid that will cover the entire top of the cauldron in case you need to snuff the fire. If in the course of your magical work you plan to light a candle inside the cauldron, you may want to first put in a layer of clean sand on the bottom of the pot, and be sure the pot will be able to contain the melted wax. To remove melted wax residue, set the pot into a sink of hot water, or boil some water in a tea kettle and pour it into a pan that the cauldron can sit in so the hot water is up to the level of the wax. After a few minutes, the wax will melt enough to pop right out with a push of your finger or a paper towel. Some spell work or ritual work may include dropping herbs into the candle flame inside the cauldron, so the flame may flare up and the wax melt very quickly. Put something under the feet of the pot before starting—or place the pot on top of a suitable pentacle—so that the heat from the cauldron will not damage or scorch the surface of whatever you are using as your altar.

Bowls

Other tools used in Circle casting and Witchcraft rituals include a pair of bowls, one for holding water and one for holding a bit of salt—sea or rock salt is preferred, or noniodized table salt—and a third dish or bowl for libations. A libation is a gift intended to honor the Divine, the Elementals, the Spirits, or the Ancestors depending on what you are doing, and consists of pouring a bit of your ritual beverage in the bowl and later adding a small piece of food to the bowl. After the Circle is opened, the contents of the libation bowl is poured onto the ground, but you can also pour it down the sink with the visualization that it will flow out to a river or ocean.

Chalice/Cup

The chalice, goblet, or cup, is placed on the Goddess side of the altar and holds the beverage used for libations and for the Cakes and Wine portion of the rituals. This cup may be of whatever material you like, but is usually of brass, pottery, silver, wood, or crystal glass. On the God side of the altar will be a small plate to hold the bread, cake, or other such food used in the libation and the Cakes and Wine portion of the rituals.

Incense Burner

An incense burner is a typical altar item as well, and may be of any variety that works for your type of incense—stick, cone, bundle, loose, powder, or resin. If using charcoal disks for burning loose, powder, or resin incense, be sure to have proper ventilation. Burning charcoal in a closed room can kill you. Since in casting the Circle, you waft incense around it, you may want to have a censer with a handle or chains to hold it by just to avoid accidentally burning your fingers.

A little sand in the bottom of a censer helps to stabilize the incense cone or charcoal disk while also protecting the container from heat. A large sea shell or a pottery bowl may be used as an incense holder, and many Witches use a feather to waft the incense smoke around the Circle, so there are many options.

Candles

Candles are frequently used in Witchcraft, and so you will need holders for them. Remember that if you are adding herbs to the candle for spell work, or even *dressing* the candle by rubbing it with an essential oil based upon the correspondence of the oil scent to the purpose of the candle, the candle will burn hot and possibly quickly. This means that you need a safe container. Some glass votive holders will break from the heat, so for magical work, the cauldron is the best place for the candle. The candles representing the Goddess and the God, and Both if a center one is used, can be tapers in individual holders or a candelabra and are usually not dressed with essential oils, but a *working candle* is the one used in spell casting and normally dressed with oil and used to burn things in its flame, so it does need a heat-resistant holder.

Pentacle

Also on the altar may be a bell, tiny or large, with a tone that appeals to you, and of such material as you like, but it is usually made of brass, silver, bronze, ceramic, or crystal. The pentacle is the flat disk with the five-pointed star in a circle engraved or painted on it, and is generally made of wood, ceramic, or metal, but may be simply drawn on a piece of paper. This tool is usually where you will set a cauldron during spell work, so it should be something that will not be affected by the generated heat.

Bolline

The bolline (*boh-leen´*) is another Witches' knife that may be placed on the altar for spell work. It is the tool used to cut and chop, and often to inscribe other tools with desired markings. It is traditionally a two-edged blade and has a white or brown handle. Unlike the athame, it is not normally used to cast the Circle or to direct energy. It does seem likely to me that this distinction is a modern one, for in the older days, a Witch probably only had one knife, so that the Circle was probably cast with the wand, and the knife was used as needed. Some Witches today follow this procedure, and use the athame to inscribe candles—and the handle of the bolline.

Besom

An important tool, also highly associated with Witchcraft, is the besom (*bess´um*), or broom. This is never used for housecleaning, but for clearing the ritual space during Circle Casting, and for ritual and spell work. Once more, in the older days, a Witch probably had only one broom, but it would be shaken in the air to clear it prior to being used to sweep a Circle, or the entire little cottage or hut would be visualized as sacred space.

Cingulum

Another tool associated with Witchcraft is the cingulum (*sing´u-lum*), which for the Self-Initiation is a nine-foot-long cord of red silk, wool, or cotton that is knotted during the ritual with your personal measurements of ankles, knees, hips, waist, chest, throat, and head, then tied with a loop on one end and a frayed knot on the other. It may be worn with the robe by passing the knotted end through the loop and securing. The color of the cord used for tying your robe may be gold without the measurement knots when symbolizing that your magical practice is that of an Energy Mover operating within a cultural tradition. Red is the color of Initiation, showing that you are working with the Elemental Powers of Nature and through the Goddess and the God, and it is the only cord that is knotted with the wearer's measurements. Black is the color designating Dedication to the Goddess and the God, thus showing that you have made a commitment to them and now work through your union with the Divine. If, or as, you pass through all these styles, you may wear just the currently appropriate color, or braid the cords together, or loosely link in three spots the separate cords that apply to you so you have a combined cingulum. I have rarely seen it worn like a bandoleer—draped from one shoulder across to the opposite hip—but this is not the typical style for Witches.

Robes

Robes are traditionally black, natural toned, or white, but may be in a color that relates to the type of ritual or spell work involved, and if tied about the waist, the cingulum is generally used.

Stang

The cingulum may also be kept on the altar, secured around the top of the staff, or wrapped around a tine of a stang, which is a wooden staff with two to three tines that is used as a staff or as a portable altar, decorated for the Sabbats, and stuck into the ground or in a stand for outdoor rituals. Like the staff, the stang may be used rather like a long wand, with one end pointed around a space for Circle casting, or with it held up during the invocation of the Elementals and the Divine in the Circle. A staff or stang may be decorated and carried as an indication of Craft association, or simply used for walking in the woods.

Basic Materials of Witchcraft

There are many other materials used in the practice of Witchcraft. Altar cloths are used to cover the altar, and may be varied according to the ritual or the season. Decorative sarongs are terrific for this purpose. You should also keep a stock of candles in various shapes and colors; cotton or silk material in a variety of colors for spell crafting, wrapping divination tools, or making poppets, dream pillows, and magical pouches; cords for knot magics, binding spells, and tying things; a variety of herbs for spell work stocked in labeled containers (glass jars are best) and kept out of direct sunlight; incenses in a variety of fragrances (to keep the scent from becoming harsh, light the incense, wait for it to glow, then blow out the flame by waving it in the air or with a feather so only the smoke results); charcoal disks for resin and powder incenses; clean glass bottles for herbs, oils, spell work, and storage of other items (rinse with spring water and sea salt to cleanse); essential oils such as rosemary, benzoin, pine, mint, lavender, and rose for anointings, dressing candles, and spell work (do not use cinnamon oil for anointing as it will burn the skin); fixed oils such as olive, sunflower, almond, and jojoba for mixing your own fragrance blends; spring water (collected at a natural spring or well, or bought prepackaged at the grocery store and rebottled in a glass container) and sea or rock salt for ritual, spell work, and cleansings; matches for lighting candles and incense; thread, yarn, or embroidery floss of various colors for tying up magical works; a variety of stones and crystals from rivers and the Earth, used in spell work, healings, balancing and aura work; acceptable beverages such as fruit juice, wine, or liqueur for rituals; musical instruments as desired to aid in meditation, spell casting, and energy raising (usually drums, sistrums, gourd rattles, bells, flutes, and cymbals are used, but also harps and other instruments); and a tile or trivet to set hot items on top of to avoid heat damage (usually the pentacle). Additionally, divination tools such as tarot cards, pendulums, and crystal balls are also kept. With tarot cards, choose a deck that appeals to you, although, over time, you may end up with a number of tarot decks that seem to pertain to the seasons or even to the types of readings being conducted. Crystal balls are usually smooth spheres without facets, but they may contain bubbles or other markings inside. The clear ones of natural quartz are very expensive, but manufactured lead crystal also works.

Preparing a Container for Magical Supplies

When you begin accumulating magical tools and supplies, you will need a place to store them when not in use. Anything from a drawer to a cabinet will suffice, using it only for magical items, and you will want to cleanse it before putting your energy-charged equipment inside. Empty it of any prior contents, wipe it out with a cloth dipped in spring water combined with sea salt, rock salt, or noniodized table salt, then place smoking incense (frankincense, copal, pine, sage, rosemary, or lavender) inside the container for thirteen minutes. Now place inside the container a small white cloth containing some more salt, tied shut with white thread. This provides cleansing energy and purification for the container. Finally, you may add for protection of your tools and equipment, a dark-brown bottle sealed with a tight lid and containing the following items:

3 black peppercorns for power

5 elderberries or hawthorn berries for the Witch's Craft

7 thorns or straight pins for protection

9 nine-inch pieces of thread or embroidery floss—
  1 each of white (for purity), black (for protection), purple
  (for spirituality), red (for power), green (for the Earth), yellow (for psychic power), orange (for attraction), blue (for
  truth), and pink (for love)

The container is now ready to hold your magical supplies.

Preparing Magical Tools with a Consecration Ritual

Your tools need to be attuned to you and the Earth for moving energy to manifest your goals. This is done through a Consecration Ritual. The Moon passes through the phases of waxing, full, waning, and new (or dark). These phases relate to the Goddess as Maiden, Mother, Crone, and Mystery, and the energy flow affects magical work just as it affects the tides of the world's seas and our own bodily fluids. The Waxing Moon ☽ is for growth and new projects, the Full Moon ○ is for completions, healing, and empowerment, the Waning Moon ☾ is for cleansings, releasings, and banishings, and the New (or Dark) Moon ● is for divinations and meditations. One of the fundamental magical traditions is to focus your work according to the phase of the Moon, and so the timing of your Consecration Ritual will be during the Full Moon.

Place three candles at the back of the altar: blue on the left side, white in the center, and orange on the right side. Light the candles and light an incense of sandalwood, sage, frankincense or other such fragrance. Set out a bowl of salt and a bowl of spring water, then lay out your ritual tools on the altar, along with a bowl of fresh water and a red votive "working candle" in a suitable container that can collect the melted wax without harm. Now light the red votive candle from the flame of the center altar candle. Since this will be the first time you will be using your tools, the first one to consecrate will be the pentacle. Hold it in your power hand (the one you favor), and say:

*I consecrate this tool of Elemental Earth (in the
names of the Goddess and the God _____ and
_____) to be used in my practice of the Craft, and I
charge this tool be made pure and ready for my use
by the manifesting power of Elemental Earth*
[sprinkle the pentacle with a little of the salt], *in-
spired by Elemental Air* [pass it through the incense
smoke], *enlivened by Elemental Fire* [pass it quickly
through the votive candle flame], *and cleansed by
Elemental Water* [sprinkle with a little water]. *This
pentacle is now by Elemental Powers bond to aid me
in my work. So Mote It Be!**

The last sentence means "so must it be" and is an emphatic
statement of affirmation and conclusion used in magic to give
power and finality to the magic being worked. A consecration is a
magical ritual, after all. Now the pentacle may be set on the altar,
and the red votive candle set in front of it. Take your other tools
and if you want, you may at this time inscribe them with whatever
symbols you desire, plus your Craft Name in a runic or other
magical alphabet, such as Theban. This step is not vital at this
time, and you may want to start using your tools before you have
decided what you want to inscribe on them. Usual symbols are a
pentagram: ⊗ ; one for the Goddess:)〇(or ᛒ or ◎—the Triple
Goddess symbol, the Runic letter Beorc, or the Lunar Spiral; one
for the God: ☿ or ᚠ or ⊕—the Horned God symbol, the Runic
letter Osa, or the Solar Cross; perhaps one for the Elementals: ⊕
or one for each Elemental: ▽ Earth, △ Air, △ Fire, and ▽
Water; one for the Sun: ☉, one for the Moon: ☽ ; and certainly
one indicating possession: ᚷ, followed by the Runic or Theban
letters of your Craft Name. Here are the Runic and Theban alphabets for writing inscriptions on your tools:

———

* *Note:* Directions for actions to be taken in a ritual are enclosed in brackets and
printed in roman type.

Theban

A	B	C	D	E	F	G	H	I	J

K	L	M	N	O	P	Q	R	S	T

U	V	W	X	Y	Z

Runic

A	B	C/K	D	E	F	G	GH	H	I

J	L	M	NG	OE	OS	P	R	S	T

TH	U	V	W	Y	Z

Once you have inscribed the tools as desired, or are otherwise ready to consecrate them, do them one at time. Hold the wand, for example, in your power hand (the hand you favor or write with) over the pentacle and say:

> *I consecrate this tool (in the names of the Goddess and the God _____ and _____) to be used in my practice of the Craft. I charge this by the manifesting strength of Elemental Earth* [sprinkle the tool with a little of the salt], *by the inspirational breath of*

Elemental Air [pass it through the incense smoke], *by the enlivening heat of Elemental Fire* [pass it quickly through the votive candle flame], *and by the cleansing purity of Elemental Water* [sprinkle with a little water].

This (name of tool) is now by Elemental Powers bond to aid me in my work, that as I will, So Mote It Be!

Do the same with each tool, then set them all on the pentacle (or touching upon the sides if you have too many to fit on the pentacle). Raise your open arms and feel energy pour into your palms as you say:

By Nature, the Sun, the Full Moon, (the Goddess and the God, _____ and _____), and the Elementals, let this tool be imbued with Power to aid me in my Craft.

Place your palms now over the tools, and feel the energy pass through your hands onto the tools as you say:

Through Nature, the Sun and the Moon, (the Lady and the Lord), and the Elementals, blessings and Power are passed through me and into these tools that they be sanctified for use in my Craft. So Mote It Be!

Kneel with both palms on the ground and say:

As what is sent returns, so do I pass the remaining Power into the Earth to be returned into the cycle of energy that flows through the Earth and the Universe.

Stand and remove the tools from the pentacle. Use them for any spell or ritual work, keeping them wrapped in a black cloth and stored in the container you prepared when they are not being used. Snuff the candles and put away the rest of the equipment, then have something to eat and drink to help return to your normal activities.

Meditation

Meditation helps you to still the tumultuous thoughts running through your head so that you can instead listen through spending some quiet time getting to know your inner self. This is not some severe, ascetic regimen requiring deprivation of food or isolation, but merely spending a little time with yourself in silence. The simplest way to enter into meditation is to sit comfortably with your feet flat on the floor and your hands on your knees or lying loosely in your lap, then let your muscles relax. Take a deep breath through your nose, hold for a few moments, exhale completely through your mouth, pause a few moments, then repeat. You only need do this two or three times to clear your lungs, then resume normal breathing. As you do the breathing exercise, relax and feel any tension you may have drain away, then ground and center. For a more soothing atmosphere, you may want to have a candle lit for focus, and a pleasant incense burning to make yourself aware that this is a different time, a time set aside for communication with yourself, with Nature, and with the Elementals. A meditation may also be undertaken while walking in Nature, simply by clearing your mind and opening your awareness only to your surroundings as you focus on the scents, sounds, sights, and textures around you, as well as the taste in the air.

If you have some question or problem that needs solving, then meditation affords a good process for looking inward without paying attention to the externals, so you can receive information from the Divine and the *Universal Unconscious*—the storehouse of universal experience accessible through altered states of consciousness. Meditation will often remove the barriers to creativity and lucid thought because you are releasing the subconscious mind to work from a perspective not open to your conscious mind. This is when you tell your conscious mind, with all its worries and uncertainties, to lie down and take a rest, so the enthusiastic energy of the subconscious mind can take over. For problem-solving meditation, you first focus on the issue you want to see resolved, then dismiss it from your mind—stop thinking about it—and proceed into the meditation. You may want to move into a visualization that takes you to a safe place from which you can move on to find a solution as presented to you by the beings you encounter in your travels, or from looking into a reflective surface at the destination (a pool, well, cauldron, etc.). Some people like to record a meditation in advance, then play it back and let their own voice guide them through it, but this is not a requirement. In silence, you can envision your safe place, then step from this to whatever travels you desire. By examining the details of your haven, you embellish it and make it real, and it is the place to which you return from your travels before returning to normal awareness.

You may want to focus on listening to the voices of Nature in your meditations. This is especially effective when done out of doors, but since the meditation involves visualization, it can be done indoors as well. In this case, you would focus on your intention, enter the meditative state, create and enter your haven, then leave it to see what you encounter from the spiritual powers of Nature. You may be opening your awareness to the energies of the land, the power, cleansing properties, or tranquillity of the sea, rivers, and springs. You may learn new things about the sky and the creatures who populate it, taking flight with eagles, owls, ravens, or insects such as the butterfly, dragonfly, or bee. Sometimes these encounters are quite vivid, and perhaps not quite what you expected, affording you with revelations and enlightenment. But throughout your meditations, you are always safe and able to stop at any time simply by wanting to be back in your safe haven where you focus on returning to normal awareness with a renewed breathing exercise.

Nature voices include not only the wisdom and messages of the animals, birds, insects, and fish, but also of the plants and trees, the waters, and the grains. Often the path through Nature is a woodland, or a mountain trek, leading you to a clear pool in which you gaze for a vision that applies to any question you may have focused on at the beginning of the meditation. Do not try to force your preconceived ideas on to a meditation. You may be quite surprised at what you learn about yourself and the issues you want to address, or you may simply be adding to your knowledge of the natural world around you. Listen to the voices of Nature and learn from them their powers and their wisdoms.

Another aspect of Nature meditation involves simply looking at the Moon in all her phases. Particularly effective is sitting and gazing at the Full Moon, letting your conscious mind grow silent as your subconscious mind opens to the meanings of the lunar appearance and color, cloud movements, rings, rays, or haloes. The Moon is the symbol of the Goddess, and through this you may reach out to her and feel her touch. The Sun is too powerful to gaze upon and will burn a hole in the retinal wall of your eye, leaving a blind spot in your field of vision if you look at it directly. This symbol of the God may be best addressed in the sunrise and sunset, through the mists, and by the light reflected on and through clouds. Shadows and the interplay of light and dark in the patterns of the woodland floor, the jeweled sparkles on the surface of water, all afford a focus for connection to the God through which you may reach out in your subconscious to learn what you may from him.

The Elementals may also be addressed in your meditations. Ask each Elemental to meet with you and show you what you need to know. Focus on the Earth, and let your subconscious mind bring into your awareness the things related through this Elemental. Then focus on Air, and do the same, then Fire, and finally Water.

Ask to see how the Elementals are part of you and how you are part of them. Ask them what powers they share, what you should seek from them, and any other question that comes to mind. See them as your loving elder siblings, your close family, and they will respond to you in kinship.

Through meditation, communing with Nature and the Elementals, you prepare yourself to hear the voices of the Goddess and the God. You will need this for when you are ready for self-initiation because you will be seeking your Witchcraft instruction from the Goddess. "The Charge of the Goddess," authored by Charles Leland and embellished by Gerald Gardner and Doreen Valiente, is found in many forms, but one key message is that the Goddess instructs her devotees, usually during Esbat Rituals of the Full Moon. When you are ready to conduct a Self-Initiation Ritual, you open the way for the Goddess to give you her instruction, and she will work with you whenever you seek her assistance and advice. If you are not ready for this, then you work your Craft through Nature and the Elementals, but even in this, the influence of the Divine is there, for they are immanent in all things.

Trusting Your Intuition

Perhaps one of the hardest things to learn is to trust your intuition. Remember that the intuitive ability is closely connected to the subconscious mind, which psychology understands recognizes events and situations before the conscious mind does—thus your conscious mind only remembers what has already occurred. In your magical work, you are free to draw upon anything that strikes your fancy, that pulls to you, because you know that all things have a relationship that you can sense.

Through trusting your intuition, you will recognize that all rituals are valid insofar as you make the necessary connection and sense the relevancy of what you are doing. What this actually means is that you are learning to move energy in a natural manner to accomplish your goals, and so your rituals may be carefully planned or spontaneous. The items used in spell work are natural since these are imbued with the essences and powers of the life-force within. You develop a feeling and respect for the powers and spirits of nature, and in working with them, you know these energies never die, but return to the Earth for redistribution once the spell is done. When using an herb for a purpose in a spell, the energy of that herb is addressed and invoked to work with you in creating the effect you desire. When you burn the herb in a candle during a ritual, you are releasing that energy to blend with your own for directing it in your magics. That energy, once focused on a goal, is then sent to work the magic. Magic is, after all, the art of creating changes.

The best way to practice magic is within the Circle, and while there are different ways to create this sacred space, what follows is the most typical in its stages of development from casting, to refreshment, to opening. All rituals and spell work are performed between the casting and the opening of the Circle, but you may want to allow time in the ritual for taking some kind of refreshment as part of the magical event. If not, then do have a bite to eat and drink afterward, and perform some routine type of work, since this will help bring you back into normal awareness. This Circle Casting Ritual has references to "the Goddess and the God," which you may change if you are working through Nature—perhaps using a substitute such as "the Elementals" or "the Power of Nature."

Casting and Opening the Circle

The Circle is made to provide you with a special place, to contain power, and to focus magic energy. You cast the Circle, perform whatever ritual or magical event is desired, be it spell casting or simply a meditation, then open the Circle and put away your tools and empty the libation bowl. The Witch can practice alone, as a

Solitary, or with a group, in a Coven, but the Witch's Rede of "If it harms none, do what you will" is accepted as valid in either situation. If you cast a Circle and then bring others into it, you cut a visualized doorway in it from left to right with your athame, let the people enter, then close it behind them from right to left with your athame. This is rather like when you were a child and played "house" with your friends. The pretend doorway was real to you as a child because you could see it through visualization—the same applies to the doorway in the Circle. You may *lock* the door by drawing a pentagram in the air at the floor when the closing motion is finished. Remember to use your Craft Name or Working Name in ritual.

The first thing you will do in casting the Circle is set up the altar. Many Witches set it up at the North for Earth, manifestation, and the Wisdom of the Goddess, but some people like to use the East, and others change according to the time of day. For the purpose of this book, we will use the North as the starting point for all activities unless otherwise noted. The altar may be decorated according to the season and type of ritual, and the general setting shown earlier can be added to or subtracted from as you desire. You can also incorporate recitations and such activities as you like in the course of your rituals.

Lay out your tools and any Craft materials you will be using in the Circle. Then prepare yourself for the ritual or magical event you have planned, bathing and robing appropriately, wearing whatever jewelry you feel is right for you. Some people wear a necklace or bracelet with a pentagram, a triple Moon, Goddess, or God design, but others do not. It is important that you wear what you feel is right for your needs. Ground and center, then starting at the North and moving deosil (many Americans pronounce this *dee'o-sil*, rather than the Gaelic *jesh'el*, but either way, this word describes a clockwise rotation or direction meant to harmonize with the Sun's movement), you sweep the area where you will be casting the Circle using a besom or perhaps a leafy branch picked up from the ground

and shaken lightly first if out of doors. A tool such as this from Nature is readily charged with energy simply by expressing your desire:
"Be my besom to sweep the sacred space of my Circle." When the
ritual is over, you simply express your appreciation to Nature for the
use of the tool and return it to the Earth. This type of experience
gives you a feel for your connection with Nature, for the tool will be
there for you, and you return it, knowing you need not hold onto
things for what is needed will come to you. As you sweep the area of
the Circle from the center outward and you state what you are
doing, for in magic the power of voice is considered very important:

> *As I sweep this Circle, may all chaotic and negative*
> *energies depart that this space be made ready for my*
> *work.*

Light the altar candles (blue-white-orange) and the incense. If
you want, you may delineate the Circle area with a cord, drawing it
in the dirt, placing flowers or other objects around the perimeter, or
you may simply visualize where it is. Candles in heat-proof containers may be placed unlit as yet at the Quarters of the Circle area, with
green for Earth at the North, yellow for Air at the East, red for Fire
at the South, and blue for Water at the West.

Ring a bell or clap three times:

> *The Circle is about to be cast and I freely stand within*
> *to greet my Lady and my Lord (the Elementals/the*
> *Powers of Nature).*

With the white center altar candle, you will either simply raise it
at each of the Quarters during the next invocation, or give the invocation and use it to light the candles you had set out at the Quarters.
You start at the North and walk deosil around the Circle, pausing at
each Quarter:

> *I call upon Light and Earth at the North to illuminate*
> *and strengthen the Circle.*

*I call upon Light and Air at the East to illuminate
and enliven the Circle.*

*I call upon Light and Fire at the South to illuminate
and warm the Circle.*

*I call upon Light and Water at the West to illumi-
nate and cleanse the Circle.*

Raise athame in power hand, facing the altar:

*I draw this Circle in the presence of the Goddess and
the God where they may come and bless their child
_____.*

Lower the athame at the North, and as you walk around the
Circle, envision a blue light shooting out from the point and
forming the Circle boundary:

*This is the boundary of the Circle, around me, above
me, below me, as a sphere is the Circle cast, and only
love shall enter and leave.*

Return to the altar and ring the bell or clap three times to show
that you are moving into the next phase of the ritual. Place the
point of the athame in the salt:

*Salt is life and purifying. I bless this salt to be used
in this sacred Circle in the Names of the Goddess
and the God, _____ and _____ (by the
Elementals/by the Powers of Nature).*

Use the athame blade to drop three tips of salt into the water
bowl and stir three times:

*Let the blessed salt purify this water that it may be
blessed to use in this sacred Circle. I consecrate and
cleanse this water in the names of the Goddess and*

*the God, _____ and _____ (by the Elementals/by
the Powers of Nature).*

Take the water bowl in one hand and sprinkle water from it as
you walk deosil around the Circle:

*I consecrate this Circle in the names of the Goddess
and the God, _____ and _____ (by the Elementals/
by the Powers of Nature). This Circle is conjured a
Circle of Power that is now purified and sealed. So
Mote It Be!*

Place the water bowl back on the altar and take the censer
around the Circle to cense it:

*Let this smoke purify this space, and may this fra-
grance be welcoming and pleasing to the energies
that manifest here.*

Now you anoint the center of your forehead, the *Third Eye*,
which is the psychic center of the brain. The sigil you use may be
the Solar Cross ⊕, a Pentagram ⊛ , the Lunar Spiral ◎ , or a
combination of these:

*I, _____ am consecrated in the names of the God-
dess and the God, _____ and _____ , (by the
Elementals/by the Powers of Nature) in this their
Circle.*

If working with others, you can open a door in the Circle now,
greeting each person by anointing them on their foreheads with
the same sigil you used, then closing the door and sealing it. Some
groups speak a password such as "Perfect Love and Perfect Trust"
before entering.

Now you are ready to invite the Elementals to the Circle, and
there are suggested envisionings for each one here, but you may

use what speaks to your heart. The Elemental representations you envision will take their positions at the Quarters, lending their energy to your work and keeping the Circle secure. Again you are starting at the North, and moving deosil around the Circle. With raised open arms, holding your wand in your power hand:

> *I call upon you, Elemental Earth, to attend this rite*
> *and guard this Circle, for as I have body and strength,*
> *we are kith and kin!* [Envision a powerful bull arriving.]

Lower your arms and go to the East; raise open arms and wand:

> *I call upon you, Elemental Air, to attend this rite*
> *and guard this Circle, for as I breathe and think, we*
> *are kith and kin!* [See an eagle soaring.]

Lower your arms and go to the South; raise open arms and wand:

> *I call upon you, Elemental Fire, to attend this rite*
> *and guard this Circle, for as I have energy and con-*
> *sume life to live, we are kith and kin!* [See a lion charging.]

Lower your arms and go to the West; raise open arms and wand:

> *I call upon you, Elemental Water, to attend this rite*
> *and guard this Circle, for as I have fluids, feelings,*
> *and a beating heart; we are Kith and Kin!* [See a leaping dolphin.]

Return to the altar and use the wand to draw in the air above the altar a cosmic lemniscate, which looks like a figure 8 laying on its side ∞, representing Infinity:

I stand between the worlds, in a place that is not a place, and in a time that is not a time.

Set the wand on the altar and raise the athame in both hands with arms up high:

Hail to the Elementals at the four Quarters! Welcome Lady and Lord (Elementals/Powers of Nature) to this rite! I stand between the worlds with love and power all around!

Lay the athame back on the altar and pour from the chalice a little beverage into the libation bowl then take a sip for yourself. Ring a bell or clap three time to show that you are now ready to begin whatever ritual, spell, meditation, or other purpose for which you created the Circle.

Conduct the Purpose for Casting the Circle

This may be spell work, meditation, divination; rituals of Sabbats/Esbats/Cakes and Wine; or Rites of Passage.

After you have finished the magical work or event you had planned, it is time to open the Circle. Hold the athame in your power hand level over the altar:

Lord and Lady (Elementals/Powers of Nature), I am blessed by your sharing this time with me; watching and guarding me, and guiding me here and in all things. I came in love and I depart in love.

Raise the athame in a salute:

Love is the Law and Love is the Bond. Merry did we meet, merry do we part, and merry will we meet again. Merry meet, merry part, and merry meet again! The Circle is now cleared. So Mote It Be!

Kiss the flat of the blade and set the athame on the altar.

Take a candle snuffer to each Quarter deosil starting at the North, or you can gently blow out the candle, thinking of the breath of life giving a blessing to each Elemental. Raise your open arms at the North:

> *Depart in peace, Elemental Earth. My blessings take with you!*

Lower your arms, snuff the candle, and envision the Elemental Power departing.

Go to the East, raise your open arms:

> *Depart in peace, Elemental Air. My blessings take with you!*

Lower your arms, snuff the candle, and envision the Elemental Power departing.

Go to the South, raise your open arms:

> *Depart in peace, Elemental Fire. My blessings take with you!*

Lower your arms, snuff the candle, and envision the Elemental Power departing.

Go to the West, raise your open arms:

> *Depart in peace, Elemental Water. My blessings take with you!*

Lower your arms, snuff the candle, and envision the Elemental Power departing.

Return to the altar and set down the snuffer, then again raise your open arms:

> *Beings and powers of the visible and invisible, depart in peace! You aid in my work, whisper in my mind, and bless me from Otherworld, and there is*

harmony between us. My blessings take with you.
The Circle is cleared.

Take your athame and go to the North Quarter, point the athame down, and walk *widdershins* (or *tuathal*, pronounced *twahth'al*, meaning "to unwind"), which is counterclockwise (North, West, South, East, and back to North) around the Circle, with the blade pointed outward toward the perimeter. Envision as you walk that the blue white light you originally sent out to cast the Circle is now being drawn back into the athame:

The Circle is open yet the Circle remains as its magi-
cal power is drawn back into me.

When you return to the North, raise the athame so the flat of the blade touches your forehead, and envision the blue light swirling around back into you.

Set the athame on the altar and balance the energy within yourself, touching your palms to the floor or ground to allow the excess energy to drain out. Now open your arms low in front of the altar:

The ceremony is ended. Blessings have been given
and blessings have been received, may the peace of
the Goddess and the God (the Elementals/the Pow-
ers of Nature) remain in my heart. So Mote It Be!

Put away all magical tools and clear the altar except for those candles or any other objects that need to burn out or sit on the pentacle for a time planned for the type of magic, such as with burning a candle spell for an hour. Pour out the contents of the libation bowl or cauldron onto the Earth, down the sink, or in the garbage as required, with the envisionment that it will be returning to the Earth. Then have something to eat and drink to help restore normal awareness.

After you are initiated and using the imagery of the Goddess and the God in your Circle casting, you may include the ritual of Cakes and Wine (or other beverage) after the magical work is completed and before opening the Circle. It would be out of place prior to this, since the ritual is itself a sacred communion with the Divine, but you can still have the food and beverage on the altar, of course, and eat and drink prior to opening the Circle if you like.

Self-Initiation

Perhaps you desire to be initiated into Witchcraft as a devotee of the Goddess and the God right away, or perhaps you would prefer to practice the Craft through Nature and the Elementals for awhile first. It does not really matter, because the Goddess and the God are already part of Nature, just as they are part of you. What does matter is your own comfort level. The Lady and Lord of Witches make no demands save that you enjoy life and take care to harm none. They know you will make mistakes, but they are patient and loving, and happy to wait for the day when you seek them out through initiation and perhaps make a solid connection with them through either a spontaneous or a ritual dedication.

The easiest way to get yourself on the path of Witchcraft with a spiritual approach that opens the Esbats and the Sabbats to you is through self-initiation. You introduce yourself to the Goddess and the God, let them know your intention to learn as much about the Craft as you can, and ask for their protection, help, love, and guidance as you walk this new path. The purpose of the following ritual is to recognize that you are entering a new phase in your life, called in Witchcraft a *Rite of Passage*, and to make personal contact with an identifiable Divinity. It is not necessary for the working of magic to have this personal relationship with Deity, but it does form a crucial part of moving from magical practice to spiritual or religious practice. All of Nature gives testament to the immanence of the Goddess and the God: through the life cycles of the plants and animals, through the seasons of the year and the phases of the Moon and Sun, and through the cycles of the Earth, both planetary and celestial. The energy that moves through all and the forms the energy takes are all manifestations of the Goddess and the God. When the time comes that you desire to connect with this great Power, you will be ready for the initiation.

For this ritual, you should have on the altar a nine-foot-long red cord of silk, wool, or cotton for the cingulum, and a small container of wine or other fruity beverage so you can *charge* (refill) your chalice after the Self-Initiation. You will be following the completed ritual with the Cakes and Wine Ritual, so also have a plate with a roll or other sort of bread or bread-like food on the altar. Traditional foods for this ceremony include fresh white bread, butter, strawberry jam, and a light rose wine or fruity beverage. If any of these foods are unappealing or create a health problem for you, feel free to substitute whatever is good for you. Go back and look at the illustration for laying out the altar to see where everything is placed. You should consider the names of the deities you will use in your ritual and in your work, or else adjust the ritual to exclude naming the Lady and the Lord. There are many books on the mythologies of ancient deities, and you may review these to see if a particular image relates to you. Cernunnos means "Horned One," and is the antlered God of the Celts, also known as Herne. Pan is the Greek goat-horned God of the wilderness, and Frey is the Norse God of Nature. Freya is the Norse Goddess of Nature, while Cerridwen is the Welsh Moon Goddess who stirs the cauldron of rebirth and knowledge. Hecate is a Thracian Moon Goddess honored in Scotland, Diana is the Moon Goddess from Rome (and known in Greece as Artemis) honored in England and Italy. These are a few of the deities familiar to Witchcraft. After casting the Circle, you are ready to begin.

Before the altar, raise your open arms:

> *Lady and Lord, I call out to you both! I hold You in honor and know that I am one with all the things of the Earth and Sky. My kin are the trees and the herbs of the fields; the animals and stones through the seas and the hills. The fresh waters and deserts are built out of you, and I am of you and you are of me.*

Lower your arms:

> *I call upon You to grant my desire. Let me rejoice in my oneness with all things and let me love the life that emanates from my Lady and my Lord into all things. I know and accept the creed; and understand that if I do not have that spark of love within me, I will never find it outside myself, for Love is the Law and Love is the Bond! And this do I honor when I give honor to the Lady and the Lord.*

Kiss your open right palm and then hold it high:

> *My Lady and my Lord, known to me as _____ and _____, I stand before You both and initiate myself to Your honor. I will defend and protect Your spark within me and seek your protection and defense of me. You are my life and I am of You. I accept and will ever abide by the ethic of the Craft, that harming none, I may do as I will. So Mote It Be!*

Take the goblet of wine and slowly pour the contents into the cauldron:

> *As this wine drains from the cup, so shall the blood drain from my body should I ever turn away from*

*the Lady and the Lord or harm those in kinship with
their love, for to do so would be to break trust, to
cast aside the love of the Goddess and the God, and
to break my own heart. Yet through Their continued
love I know They would heal my heart and spirit
that I might again journey through the cauldron of
rebirth to embrace the love They freely give. So Mote
It Be!*

Dip the forefinger of your power hand into the anointing oil and draw the sigil of the Solar Cross ⊕ over your Third Eye in the center of your forehead; then draw the sigil of the Pentagram ⊛ over your heart in the center of your chest; and then draw the Sacred Triangle ▽ representing the Triple aspects of both the Goddess and the God, touching solar plexus (lower abdomen below the navel), right breast, left breast, and back to solar plexus.

Take the cord now and use it to measure and mark with a knot each place: ankles, knees, hips, waist, chest, throat, and head (forehead), then make a loop and knot on one end and fray the other end:

*This is the measure of myself, my cingulum to tie my
robe, and to bind me to my Craft. By this cord am I
known.*

Tie the cord around your waist, passing the frayed end through the loop and securing, then raise your arms, opened wide:

*As a sign of my chosen new life and initiation into
the Craft, I take for myself a new name. As I study
the Craft that I may be worthy to be called Witch, I
shall be known as _____ . Know now my name, my
Lady and my Lord, and see me as this name and a
part of You both. So Mote It Be!*

Lower your arms and meditate for a time on this new path begun, and on being in the Old Religion. Let the feelings flow out of your body and let the power and love of the Goddess and the God enter in. Raise both your hands:

> *I am blessed by the Goddess and the God, known to me as _____ and _____ , by Your attendance at my Initiation! Know that I am Your child, _____ , and receive me into Your guidance!*

Refill the chalice with some more beverage from the container on the altar, pour a small amount into the libation bowl, take a sip, then raise the chalice:

> *I call the blessings of the Goddess and the God upon me!*
> *Blessed be my feet that bring me on my path.*
> *Blessed be my knees that support me before the Lady and the Lord.*
> *Blessed be my sexuality that honors life.*
> *Blessed be my breast that holds my heart true to my path.*
> *Blessed be my lips that speak the sacred names.*
> *Blessed be my eyes that see the beauty of Divine love.*
> *Blessed be my mind that seeks the wisdom of the Goddess and the God.*

Set the cup on the altar and proceed to the Cakes of Wine Ritual.

Cakes and Wine

Ring the bell or clap three times. With your feet spread and your open arms raised before the altar:

> *I acknowledge my needs and offer my appreciation*
> *to that which sustains me! May I ever remember the*
> *blessings of the Lady and the Lord.*

Bring your feet together and hold the cup in your left hand and the athame in your right hand. Slowly lower the point of the athame into the cup:

> *As the Divine Male joins the Divine Female for the*
> *benefit of both and for us all, let the fruits of Their*
> *Sacred Union promote life, love, and joy. Let the Earth*
> *be fruitful and let her bounty be spread throughout all*
> *lands.*

Set the athame on the altar and pour a libation into the libation bowl or cauldron. Now touch point of athame to the bread/cake in the offering dish:

> *This food is the blessing of the Lady and the Lord*
> *given to me. As I have received, may I offer food for*
> *the body, mind, and spirit to those who seek such of*
> *me.*

Eat the ritual meal and finish the beverage. In a ritual with other people present, you divide the meal and beverage with them all. When finished:

> *As I have enjoyed these gifts of the Goddess and the*
> *God, may I remember that without Them I would*
> *have nothing. So Mote It Be!*

Now you are ready to open the Circle as already shown.

The Esbat Rituals

By introducing yourself to the Divine, you can seek their assistance in your Craft education. The Goddess is the one who teaches through intuition, and to meet with her, you need to understand and connect with the energy flow of the Moons that represent her psychic, intuitive power in their various capacities. After introducing yourself through initiation, and stating your desire to learn about the Craft, you need to start paying more attention to that still inner voice, and begin celebrating the Esbats that honor her. The Esbats may be observed by a Witch who is not initiated, but this would be through observing the Moon, enjoying the beauty of the Moon in Nature, and applying the lunar energies to spell work. But to perform the rituals of the Esbats requires that you accept the Goddess as a partner in your Craft and in spirituality.

There are rituals for both the Full Moon and for the New Moon, but while most Witches celebrate the Full Moon Esbat, not all celebrate the New Moon Esbat, preferring to see this period as a time for introspection and meditation. The candles may be blue, white, and orange or green, white, and red for the Esbats. Incenses may have a rich aroma or be of sandalwood, frankincense, or bay. Since the Full Moon is a great time for conducting spell work, be sure to have all the necessary materials on the altar, as well as the food and beverage for the Cakes and Wine portion of the Ritual. Once you have cast the Circle, you may conduct the Esbat Ritual for the appropriate lunar phase as shown:

Esbat Introduction

With open arms, raise the wand in greeting:

> *I, _____ , who am Your child, stand between the*
> *worlds and call upon my Lady and my Lord, _____*
> *and _____ , to hold communion with me.*

Ring the bell or clap three times:

"If it harms none, do what you will," thus runs the Witch's Rede. Once more I affirm my joy of life and feelings for the Lady and the Lord. I honor the God and the Goddess, _____ and _____ , for the favors They have bestowed upon me, and ask Their blessings upon me.

Set the water bowl on the pentacle and hold the athame over it:

Great Mother, bless this creature of Water and of Earth to Your service. May I always remember the cauldron waters of rebirth and the many forms and beings of the blessed Earth. Of Water and Earth am I.

Hold up the water bowl in both hands:

Great Mother, I honor You!

Set the water bowl back in its proper place on the altar, then set the censer on the pentacle and hold your athame over it:

Great Father, bless this creature of Fire and of Air to Your service. May I always remember the sacred fire that dances within every creation and may I always hear the voices of the Divine. Of Fire and Air am I.

Hold up the censer with both hands:

Great Father, I honor You!

Set the censer back in its proper place on the altar, then hold up the beverage chalice:

Power and Grace; Beauty and Strength are in the Lady and the Lord both. Patience and Love; Wisdom and Knowledge. I honor You both!

Pour a libation from the chalice into the libation bowl or caul-dron and take a sip.

For the Full Moon

Face the altar with raised open arms and feet spread apart:

> *Behold the Great Lady, Who travels the sky; the stars*
> *shine around Her and light up the night.*

Pick up the wand and hold it raised over the altar. If outside or where the Moon can reflect on the surface of water in a cauldron, you can do a Drawing Down of the Moon, charging the water and using it for scrying (covered in Chapter Six), or otherwise, gaze at the Moon if possible or envision how it appears:

> *Lovely Lady known by so many names, but known*
> *to me as _____ , with the Lord, _____ , at Your side,*
> *honor and reverence I give to You and I invite You to*
> *join with me on this, Your special night. Descend,*
> *my Lady, and speak with Your child _____ .*

Listen for her to speak to you, or if you needed guidance on a matter, she will instruct you. Set the wand back on the altar and proceed to any spell work, consecrations, divinations, etc. When completed, raise your arms at the altar:

> *You are the Mother of All. Maiden, Mother, and*
> *Crone—you are at life's beginning and at its end.*
> *You dwell within us all for you are Life and Love,*
> *and thus do you make me Life and Love. Love is the*
> *Law and Love is the Bond. So Mote It Be!*

You now continue on to Cakes and Wine and the opening of the Circle.

For the New Moon

Stand in front of the altar with your head bowed and your arms crossed over your chest as you chant the name of the Goddess, proceeding when ready:

> *As _____ are you known to me, Great Lady. This is the Moon of my Lady as Crone; Lady of Darkness, of Wisdom, of Mysteries shown.*
>
> *The Wheel turns through birth, death, and rebirth, and every end is a new beginning. You are the passage from life to life. You are She who is at the beginning and the end of all time. You, with Your Lord _____ at Your side, abide in us all. So Mote It Be!*

Enjoy a moment of reverent silence to consider the mysteries of the Goddess who is both life and passage, and your special closeness to the Goddess of the Witches. Appropriate spell work, meditation, or divination may be conducted before going on to the Cakes and Wine Ritual and opening the Circle.

4

Celebrating the Sabbats

The Eight Sabbat Rituals

The Sabbats may be observed by a Witch who is not initiated, but mainly through special activities, home decorations, and a traditional meal, since the rituals relate specifically to the Goddess and the God. For the person who practices the Craft under the umbrella of a mainstream religion, the holidays will be those defined by that religion and embellished personally to show the connection with Nature. For the person who practices Witchcraft without religious reference, simply being aware of the changing of the seasons is sufficient and may be enhanced through familiar seasonal activities from planting a garden to harvesting, hunting, picking wild berries to make pies; attending country fairs or rodeos; engaging in egg hunts, tree decorating, and present exchanging; and eating seasonal foods from ham or stuffed turkey to fruitcake or cornbread. For the person who has performed the Self-Initiation Ritual, your practice of Witchcraft is now also your religion. While you may choose to limit your Sabbats to the former types of activities, you may instead use these intentionally to augment the ritual celebration of each Sabbat. These eight holidays offer you the opportunity to honor the Goddess and the God at the turning of the seasons and in accordance with Their mythic progression through the year.

The Sabbat Rituals may also be embellished as much as you desire, with selected readings of poems or other pertinent material you feel fits the season, meditations, divinations, or supplemented with a Re-affirmation of Oath Ritual. Holiday decorations around the home and special activities may be coordinated with Sabbat Rituals, so you have many options to choose from. For the rituals, you first cast the Circle as usual, perform the ritual, have Cakes and Wine, and open the Circle. Spell work is usually not performed with Sabbats, but this is not a hard and fast rule. Meditations and divinations may be part of your Sabbat activities, performed either during the ritual or afterward.

Sometimes the Full Moon or New Moon fall on a Sabbat, in which case you have the option of celebrating the Esbat first, then the Sabbat, followed by Cakes and Wine, and opening of the Circle. You may play around with the contents of the two rituals to blend them together in a way that makes sense to you. You could skip the Esbat and only celebrate the Sabbat, if desired, or do each at separate times during the day. As long as you harm none, there is a lot of leeway in how you do things.

As usual, you will prepare everything prior to casting the Circle so you are ready. Seasonal decorations around the altar or Circle provide additional ambiance, and the candle colors and recommended incense for the altar will be described for each Sabbat.

The Yule Sabbat — December 21

Use red-green-red for the altar candles, and choose an incense of bay, bayberry, frankincense, myrrh, rosemary, or sage. The altar and Circle may be decorated with any of the following: holly, evergreens, pine cones, oak leaves, ivy, mistletoe, or blessed thistle. Traditional foods for the Yule Sabbat include nuts, fruits mixed in a fruitcake or plum pudding, pork, game, or fowl dishes, and a wassail (add together in a punchbowl: 1 liter cranberry juice, 1 liter ginger ale, and 1 pint orange sherbet, for a frothy nonalcoholic beverage, or add champagne or rum). Place a few ash-wood twigs in the cauldron. If you cannot find ash wood, pine may be used as a substitute. Familiar activities include decorating the Yule Tree; and opening presents under the tree on Solstice Morning.

Ring a bell or clap three times, then raise your open arms:

> *Blessed are the Lord and the Lady who turn the mighty Wheel of the Year. Welcome the Yule for the turning point of Winter is here at last. The end of the Solar Year has come; a New Solar Year has begun. The Holly King departs as the Oak King is born; the Crone delivers Him of the Mother. Hail the Mystery of Sage and Babe, of Crone and Mother!*

Pick up the wand and hold it high:

> *This day is a new beginning, and I send my power forth to join with the energies of the Sun God, that the Sun's rebirth rekindles my strength as the rays rekindle the warmth of the Earth* [feel your energies merge with the Sun's and return to fill you with cleansing warmth; release the excess].

Set the wand on the altar; then use the middle candle to light the kindling in the cauldron:

> *This new fire is lit to bid farewell to the Dark Lord of the Solar Night and greet the newborn Lord of Light, seen in the rebirth of the Sun. May my power be added to the strength of the newborn Lord, and His to mine.*

Raise high the athame in both hands:

Hail to the God of Light and Joy! Hail the movement of Time Eternal! The Holly King leaves with gifts for all as symbols of His love. His eight great stags carry His sleigh to the realm of snow and ice, where, in His wisdom, He awaits the next turning of the Solstice Wheel. Hail the passage of the Sage and His rebirth at Yule! Hail the God Eternal!

Set down the athame and ring the bell or clap three times.

The Holly King has left; may I hold His wisdom in my heart. The Oak King has come; may I hold His promise in my soul. Through the stages of life, death, and rebirth am I shown the Mystery, for there is no death, only passage, and the God holds the torch to light the way. God of Light and Joy, held within the Mother's arms, the radiance of Your face lifts my spirit in the dark of Winter, and brings me comfort and peace. May the Yule bring Light, and may all good enter here. Good health, good cheer, good fortune in the coming year! That as I will, So Mote It Be!

Proceed to Cakes and Wine, and open the Circle.

The Imbolc Sabbat
February 2

Use pale blue-white-pale blue or all white candles for the altar, and choose an incense of vanilla, basil, bay, benzoin, celandine, pear, or other such scent. The altar and Circle may be decorated with any of the following: white, yellow, or light blue flowers, angelica, or myrrh. Place your besom on the altar, as well as a small dish of rosemary, a small dish of bay leaf, and a white votive candle in the cauldron. Traditional foods are from dairy products and spiced with onion, leek, shallot, garlic, or containing raisins or olives, with bread puddings and creamy soups being typical. The beverage may be a spiced wine or spiced apple cider. This ritual includes an optional Re-affirmation of the Oath of Initiation, so be sure to have a libation bowl large enough to hold the contents of the chalice, and also a container of beverage to charge (refill) the cup for Cakes and Wine.

Ring a bell or clap three times, then raise your open arms:

> *This is the Midwinter Feast of Lights. The Spring lies within sight, the Earth quickens, the milk of ewes flows, and the seed is prepared for sowing. Now does the midwife Crone place the Infant God of Light in the arms of the cleansed Mother, and departs to reunite with the Holly King in the land of Snow and Ice, that the seasons unfold once more.*

Ring a bell or clap five times, then pick up the besom with both hands:

> *With my besom in my hand I sweep out that which is no longer needed, purifying my surroundings and preparing for new growth.*

Use the besom to sweep the Circle deosil, with outward motions:

> *Clear out the old and let the new enter. Life starts anew at this time of cleansing.*

Place the besom back on the altar and light the cauldron candle. Drop into the flame a little of the rosemary and bay:

> *I call upon the power of these herbs that their scent now released in this cauldron's fire purify me, my*

surroundings, and the tools of my Craft. With this
rite I am re-affirmed in my Craft and made ready
for the renewal of life in the coming of Spring.

Carefully wave the brushy end of the besom over the cauldron:

May this besom be cleansed that nothing cast out of
the Circle now and in the coming year return with it
or cling to it. So Mote It Be!

Lean the besom against the altar and pass other tools of the Craft across the cauldron:

These are the tools of my Craft; may they be purified
and cleansed for use in the coming year. So Mote
It Be!

The Re-Affirmation of Oath:

Raise your open arms before the altar:

As I have purified all within this Circle, I am now
ready to re-affirm my commitment to my Craft and
to my Lady and my Lord. I call out to You both to
know that I hold You in honor. I know that I am one
with all the things of the Earth and Sky. My kin are
the trees and the herbs of the fields; the animals
and stones through the seas and the hills. The fresh
waters and deserts are built out of you, and I am of
You and You are of me.

Lower your arms:

I call upon You hear my re-affirmation of my oath
and know that I rejoice in my oneness with all
things and that I love the life that emanates from
my Lady and my Lord into all things. I know and

accept the creed; and understand that if I do not
have that spark of love within me, I will never find
it outside myself, for Love is the Law and Love is the
Bond! And this do I honor when I give honor to the
Goddess and the God.

Kiss your open right palm and then hold it high:

My Lady and my Lord, known to me as _____ and
_____ , I stand before You both and re-affirm myself
to Your honor. I will defend and protect Your spark
within me and seek Your protection and defense of
me. You are my life and I am of You. I accept and
will ever abide by the ethic of the Craft, that harm-
ing none, I may do as I will. As I Will, So Mote It Be!

Take the goblet of wine and slowly pour the contents into the
cauldron:

As this wine drains from the cup, so shall the blood
drain from my body should I ever turn away from
the Lady and the Lord or harm those in kinship with
Their love, for to do so would be to break trust, to
cast aside the love of the Goddess and the God, and
to break my own heart. Yet I do not fear, for even so,
through Their continued love I know They would
heal my heart and spirit that I might again journey
through the cauldron of rebirth to embrace the love
They freely give. So Mote It Be!

Dip the forefinger of your power hand into the anointing oil
and draw the sigil of the Solar Cross ⊕ over your Third Eye in
the center of your forehead; then draw the sigil of the Pentagram
⊛ over your heart in the center of your chest; and then draw the
Sacred Triangle ▽ representing the Triple aspects of both the

Goddess and the God, touching solar plexus (lower abdomen below the navel), right breast, left breast, and back to solar plexus.

Refill the chalice with more beverage from the container on the altar, pour a small amount into the libation bowl, take a sip, then raise the chalice:

> *I call the blessings of the Goddess and the God upon*
> *   me!*
> *Blessed be my feet that bring me on my path.*
> *Blessed be my knees that support me before the Lady*
> *   and the Lord.*
> *Blessed by my sexuality that honors life.*
> *Blessed be my breast that holds my heart true to my*
> *   path.*
> *Blessed be my lips that speak the sacred names.*
> *Blessed be my eyes that see the beauty of Divine*
> *   love.*
> *Blessed be my mind that seeks the wisdom of the*
> *   Goddess and the God.*

Proceed to Cakes and Wine, then open the Circle.

The Ostara Sabbat
March 21

Use light green or light green-pink-light green altar candles, and choose an incense of jasmine, rose, violets, tansy, cinquefoil, celandin, or a lightly floral fragrance. The Circle and altar may be decorated with any of the following: wild flowers, daffodil, dogwood, honeysuckle, iris, crocus, lily, strawberry, or acorn. Have on the altar a bundle of wildflowers and an earthenware or wooden bowl containing some soil. Place a large seed on the pentacle. Have a piece of parchment or vellum paper, ink, and writing tool on the altar. Traditional foods are those containing seeds and sprouts, such as poppy seed or sesame seed rolls, salads, hard-boiled eggs (with colored or decorated shells), yellow cake with poppy seeds, banana nut bread, and ham, roast beef, or roast poultry. Beverages may be a sweet or honeyed wine, light fruit juice, or fruit liqueur.

Ring a bell or clap three times, then raise your open arms:

> *I call upon me the Blessings of the Ancient Ones as merry do we meet at this Springtime Rite. Lady and Lord, hear your child, _____ , for I am here to celebrate with You and for You as we greet the Spring together!*

Sprinkle the wildflowers deosil around the inside perimeter of the Circle:

> *Lady and Lord, frolic and play; stir up the creatures along Your way!*

Ring a bell or clap three times:

> *Springtime is when we sow the seed; it is the time for me to plant what I want to grow. This season brings hope and joy; expectations for desires realized; and inspiration for new ideas. My life is brought into balance and I am reborn, resurrected, with the Earth's renewal. I welcome thee, Ostara, beautiful Spring!*

Place the bowl of soil on the pentacle; focus on seeing the seed as an idea or thing to be manifested; then ring a bell or clap 1 time. Write on the paper the seed idea or thing desired. Light the parchment from the center candle and drop the burning ash onto the soil in the bowl, using the athame to mix it into the soil:

Lady and Lord, let this soil be prepared and fertile to receive the seed of my desire, that here it may grow and prosper, to ripen and bear fruit, as it grows and prospers in my mind and heart to reach maturity and fruition.

Raise the wand with open arms and dance or skip deosil three times around the Circle to raise energy, then stop at the altar with the wand still held up:

By the power instilled in this raised wand will the seed be planted in the ready soil. Blessed Be the Wand of Spring and Blessed Be the Earth that receives it!

Kiss the tip of the wand, envisioning the energy transferring into it. With the tip of the wand, make an indentation in the center of the soil, visualizing the energy entering the soil, then set the wand down. Hold up the seed, focus energy into it and *know* the idea will be manifested as the plant grows. Place the seed into the furrow and close the soil over it.

This seed is planted in the Mother's womb to be part of the Earth, of Life, and of me. Let this seed and what it represents grow to manifestation. That as I will, So Mote It Be!

Ring a bell or clap three times, then proceed to Cakes and Wine, and open the Circle. Afterward, transplant the seed and soil into the garden, a large flower pot, or other suitable place.

The Beltane Sabbat
May 1

Use dark green or dark green-white-dark green candles on the altar, and choose an incense of lilac, almond, frankincense, marigold, meadowsweet, woodruff, or similar fragrance. The Circle and altar may be decorated with any of the following: daisy, lilac, rose, primrose, bluebells, angelica, ivy, hawthorn flowers, green herbs, or wildflowers. Have a dark-green votive candle inside the cauldron, and a bowl with a small amount of woodruff. In separate (labeled) dishes or bowls, have wood chips from birch, oak, rowan (mountain ash), willow, hawthorn, hazel, apple, vine, and fir on the altar (look for these in Nature, home-improvement centers, or craft, lumber, or occult supply stores). Traditional foods include things flavored with flowers, such as cookies made with rose extract and custards containing marigold or nasturtium, spiced pears, raisin cinnamon bread, bread with almonds and almond paste, and almond or oatmeal cakes. Beverages may be fruit juice, floral flavored ice tea, fruity wine, wine flavored with rose or nasturtium petals, a dandelion wine, or a May wine.

> *The Goddess of Summer walks through the land with the God of the Forest, and the dark time of Winter is behind me.*

Ring a bell or clap seven times:

> *The animals breed and the plants pollinate, as the May Queen and the Green Man bestow Their blessings upon the Earth and her creatures. I, who am their child, _____ , rejoice with Them and ask that their happy union become an example for all humanity to live in love and harmony.*

Light the votive candle in the cauldron:

> *The dark days are cleared away that the May Day can now begin!*

Drop some of the woodruff into the votive flame:

> *May the light of Beltane fire bring happiness and*
> *peace, and may the victory of the King of the Wild-*
> *wood come into my life that I may always dwell in*
> *the joy of the Lady and the Lord. So Mote It Be!*

Drop a pinch of each type of wood chip into the cauldron flame during this chant:

> *I burn thee birch to honor the Goddess;*
> *And now add thee oak to honor the God.*
> *Thou rowan I add for a magical life;*
> *And add thee willow to celebrate death.*
> *Thou hawthorn I burn for Fairies near me;*
> *Thou hazel I burn for wisdom you bring.*
> *I add thee good apple to bring to me love;*
> *And thou sweet vine whose fruit brings me joy.*
> *Fir, you are added to remember rebirth;*
> *Your sweet savor sings of immortality.*
> *My blessings I give to all of thee;*
> *And thy blessings I call from thee upon me;*
> *That as I will, So Mote It Be!*

While the wood chips burn raise the chalice in both hands:

> *I greet the time of unions and give honor to the Lord*
> *and the Lady for their fruitfulness!*

Pour a little beverage into the libation bowl, then take a sip from the cup and set it back on the altar. Cover the cauldron so the fire is extinguished.

Ring a bell or clap three times, then proceed to Cakes and Wine and open the Circle.

The Litha Sabbat
June 21

Use dark blue-white-dark blue or all dark blue candles for the altar, and choose an incense of lavender, mugwort, thyme, vervain, musk, or patchouli. The Circle and altar may be decorated with any of the following: pine, rose, wisteria, larkspur, hemp, or St. Johnswort. Have on the altar a bowl containing a mixture of a small amount of these nine herbs: betony or basil, chamomile, fennel or lavender, lemon balm or carnation, mullein, rue, St. Johnswort, thyme, and vervain. Also have on the altar a small quantity of water in the cauldron, and a red votive candle that will later sit within the cauldron. Leave the water bowl partially empty to receive water from the cauldron. The Circle and altar may be decorated with summer flowers and fruit. Traditional foods include cold cooked meats or fried chicken, potato salad with hard-boiled eggs, sweet breads, herbed bread, and pastries. The beverage may be a red wine, honey mead, a light or summer wine, or herbal Sun tea. This Sabbat Ritual includes an optional Re-affirmation of the Oath of Initiation, so if using this, be sure to have a libation bowl large enough to hold the contents of the chalice, and also a container of beverage to charge the cup for Cakes and Wine.

Ring a bell or clap three times, then raise your open arms:

> *I celebrate Life on this Midsummer day! Sadness is cast aside and joy flows within as the High Summer now begins.*

Light the red votive candle from the center candle and hold it in your right hand:

> *The Light of the Sun, the God of Life, shines round me and in me for all the world to see.*

Set the votive on the pentacle, then, with fingertips, sprinkle water from the cauldron on the altar:

The Lord and Lady of the Greenwood have made their pact. The Oak King turns His face to that of the Holly King so He may wed the Queen and pass into Her tender care. The Lord rises into the Lady and prepares to descend into the corn, in both ways to be born again of the Mother.

Pour the water from the cauldron into the blessed water bowl, then set the votive inside the cauldron and set the cauldron on the pentacle:

Life entering the Lady's care is sanctified and purified in Her love.

Ring a bell or clap nine times, then raise your open arms:

As the Sun moves on his course, so the course of Life moves closer to Death that Life may come again. Soon will the Lord of the Corn move into His realm to become the Lord of Shadows, but now in the fullness of Summer, He shares the joy of His life and His love with all of the Earth.

Hold your athame over the votive candle:

As the God and Goddess share Their light and life with me, so do I share with others and offer comfort as is meet.

Stir the herbal mixture with your athame, then add the herbs to the votive candle:

I call upon the powers imbued in these herbs that the Midsummer Fire be empowered. Herbs of the

Earth: symbols of Otherworld, of the planets, of Life, and of Love, your scent fills the air and drives away care.

Rest your palms on the altar:

Lord and Lady, You fill my life with Your bountiful love and gifts! I call upon You both for Your continued blessings, and I offer my petition to You both that Your love and caring remain with me always. Bless me now and receive my blessing, my appreciation for life, for love, for joy, and for that spark that brings me to You. May I pass this joy to others. So Mote It Be!

You may now do the Re-affirmation of Oath Ritual, if desired, or proceed to Cakes and Wine, then open the Circle.

The Re-Affirmation Of Oath:

Hold the wand up in your power hand:

At this time of Midsummer joy, I re-affirm my oath of love for my Lord and my Lady and commitment to my Craft. I call out to You both to know that I hold you in honor. I know that I am one with all the things of the Earth and Sky. My kin are the trees and the herbs of the fields; the animals and stones through the seas and the hills. The fresh waters and deserts are built out of you, and I am of you and you are of me.

Lower your arms:

Hear now my re-affirmation of my oath and know that I rejoice in my oneness with all things and that

I love the life that emanates from my Lady and my
Lord into all things. I know and accept the creed;
and understand that if I do not have that spark of
love within me, I will never find it outside myself,
for Love is the Law and Love is the Bond! And this
do I honor when I give honor to the Goddess and the
God.

Kiss your open right palm and then hold it high:

My Lady and my Lord, known to me as _____ and
_____ , I stand before You both and re-affirm myself
to Your honor. I will defend and protect Your spark
within me and seek Your protection and defense of
me. You are my life and I am of you. I accept and
will ever abide by the ethic of the Craft, that harm-
ing none, I may do as I will. As I Will, So Mote It Be!

Take the goblet of wine and slowly pour the contents into the
cauldron:

As this wine drains from the cup, so shall the blood
drain from my body should I ever turn away from
the Lady and the Lord or harm those in kinship with
Their love, for to do so would be to break trust, to
cast aside the love of the Goddess and the God, and
to break my own heart. Yet I do not fear, for even so,
through Their continued love I know They would
heal my heart and spirit that I might again journey
through the cauldron of rebirth to embrace the love
They freely give. So Mote It Be!

Dip the forefinger of your power hand into the anointing oil
and draw the sigil of the Solar Cross ⊕ over your Third Eye in
the center of your forehead; then draw the sigil of the Pentagram

✪ over your heart in the center of your chest; and then draw the Sacred Triangle ▽ representing the Triple aspects of both the Goddess and the God, touching solar plexus (lower abdomen below the navel), right breast, left breast, and back to solar plexus.

Refill the chalice with some more beverage from the container on the altar, pour a small amount into the libation bowl, take a sip, then raise the chalice:

> *I call the blessings of the Goddess and the God upon me!*
>
> *Blessed be my feet that bring me on my path.*
>
> *Blessed be my knees that support me before the Lady and the Lord.*
>
> *Blessed be my sexuality that honors life.*
>
> *Blessed be my breast that holds my heart true to my path.*
>
> *Blessed be my lips that speak the sacred names.*
>
> *Blessed be my eyes that see the beauty of Divine love.*
>
> *Blessed be my mind that seeks the wisdom of the Goddess and the God.*

Proceed to Cakes and Wine, then open the Circle.

The Lughnassadh Sabbat
August 1

Use yellow- or wheat-colored candles for the altar, and choose an incense of frankincense, copal, myrrh, patchouli, heather, or a similar scent. The altar and Circle may be decorated with any of the following: acacia flowers, ears of corn, hollyhock, myrtle, oak leaves, stalks of wheat or barley, or summer flowers. Place a loaf of whole, cracked-wheat, or multigrain bread on the altar. Traditional foods include multigrain bread, blackberry pie, and wine or beer.

Ring a bell or clap three times, then raise your open arms:

*I celebrate this day the First Harvest, the Festival of
Bread, for this is the marriage day of the Sun and
the Earth.*

Chant or sing while dancing around the Circle:

*Dance, dance, wherever you may be;
When you dance with the Lord, He will dance
    with thee.
Turn, turn, a circle you may form;
And the Lord of the Dance is the Lord of the Corn!*

Stop at the altar; raise your open arms to continue singing or
chanting:

*Down, down, into the Earth He'll go;
Giving life to the grain that in Spring we'd sown.
He rules the Shadowland 'til Yule;
When His Sun is reborn and He joins us anew!*

Ring a bell or clap seven times:

*Great is the power of the God of the Sun and the
Goddess of the Earth, from Whom spring all life!*

Hold your wand over the bread:

*The harvest of the corn that sustains us is brought
through death and rebirth. The Lord of the Corn
leaves the side of the Earth Mother that His power
may be passed into the land for His children to live.
Blessed Be the God of the Corn, Whose love for His
children knows no bounds! In the Land of Shadows
will He abide with the Lady as Crone, awaiting the
time of His joyous rebirth.*

Touch the bread with your wand:

> *May the God, _____ , bless this bread that I eat in*
> *the honor of the cycle of life that created it and me.*

Tear off a small portion of the bread and drop it into the libation bowl, then eat a bite of the bread (the rest may be saved for Cakes and Wine or served to others).

Hold with palms up, raise arms to level over the altar:

> *My Lord and my Lady, _____ and _____ , I am*
> *blessed by Your gifts from the soil. These first grains*
> *are the promise of life to come. Let the power of the*
> *Goddess and the God be in me at this time and*
> *throughout the year, that I never forget that I am*
> *one with the All, the Divine in balance. So Mote*
> *It Be!*

Ring a bell or clap three times. Proceed to Cakes and Wine, then open the Circle.

The Mabon Sabbat
September 21

Use brown, russet orange, or burgundy red candles for the altar, and choose an incense of pine, sage, sweetgrass, myrrh, marigold, thistle, benzoin, or other such scent. The altar and Circle may be decorated with any of the following: asters, mums, ferns, honeysuckle, pine, rose, acorns, gourds, corn sheaves, milkweed, maple and oak leaves. Have a nutbread in a dish on the altar, and canned goods to donate on or beside the altar. Traditional foods include smoked meats, poultry with fruit and nut stuffing, hearty bean soup, squash pies, nut bread, and apple or rhubarb pie. Beverages may be juices from vine fruits, and currant or blackberry wine.

Ring a bell or clap three times, then raise your open arms:

This day I celebrate the Second Harvest, that of fruits, nuts and the vines, and I remember those who struggle without. As I accept the gifts of the Lord and the Lady so do I pass along what I may to those who have need.

Ring a bell or clap three times:

The Wheel of the Year is ever turning, through Sun Tides and Moon Tides, through seasons and harvests, for plants and for people; for all life moves within the Wheel of the Year from life to death to life again. The balance and the harmony of the dance of life is the spiral dance of Energy Eternal, lead by the God guiding us.

He yearly travels the path of Nature on our behalf that we know and not fear the cycles of our being, for balance and harmony in the motion of life are His truths.

Hold up the plate of nut bread and chalice of beverage:

I ask the blessing of the Lady and the Lord, _____ and _____ , upon this food, that the harvest be bountiful.

Ring a bell or clap three times:

The Lord of Shadows rules in his Shadowland, yet his love holds true, and with him my own dance will one day move the Other Way. As this harvest season moves onward to the last harvest, I call upon the Lady and the Lord to bless this beautiful season and my life within it, that my life may be the harvest of the Goddess and the God.

Take the wand to walk deosil around the Circle, pausing to honor each of the Elementals at the Quarters with raised open arms, starting at the North, then lowering arms, and continuing to the next Elemental until returned to the altar:

At the North:

> *Hail to thee, Elemental Earth! Your steadfastness helps me to maintain the things of my home, my health, my security, and my comfort! We are kith and kin, and I honor you!*

At the East:

> *Hail to thee, Elemental Air! Your inspiration helps me to learn, understand, and express my creativity! We are kith and kin, and I honor you!*

At the South:

> *Hail to thee, Elemental Fire! Your energy helps me with the drive to accomplish my goals and fuels my body and mind! We are kith and kin, and I honor you!*

At the West:

> *Hail to thee, Elemental Water! Your gentle flow helps me maintain calm and balance in my relationships with others, and opens my psychic awareness and intuitive powers! We are kith and kin, and I honor you!*

At the altar, touch the canned goods with the wand:

> *In the names of the Lord and the Lady, and with the aid of the Elementals, I bless these fruits of the harvest for those who are in need. I offer aid and*

comfort to those whose needs arise throughout
the turning of the Wheel. May the Goddess and the
God, _____ and _____ , bless these offerings, the
one who gives and the one who receives. So Mote
It Be!

Ring a bell or clap three times. Proceed to Cakes and Wine, then open the Circle.

The Samhain Sabbat
October 31

Use black-orange-black or all black or all orange candles for the altar, and chose an incense of patchouli, sage, mullein, heather, or myrrh. The altar and Circle may be decorated with any of the following: autumn flowers, oak leaves, apples, acorns, small pumpkins, Indian corn, small gourds, straw, ferns, flax, dittany of Crete. Have a black votive candle inside the cauldron, and on the altar place a piece of parchment or vellum paper with a list of weaknesses or bad habits you want to banish written on it. On the altar have also a white votive candle, a small dish of loose heather, and an apple. Traditional beverages are dark wine, beer, or apple cider. Typical foods include pumpkin pie, squashes, corn on the cob, game birds with savory stuffing, and taffy apples. A Dumb Supper of bread, salt, and cider or beer may be set at an extra place at the dinner table to honor the ancestors during the family meal. Another version of the Dumb Supper involves doing everything by candlelight in silence and backward (walking backward around the table as you set it, eating the meal starting with dessert, and setting the bread, salt, and beer at an empty seat), invoking in silence the presence of the spirits, farewelling them in silence, followed by divinations. A jack-o'-lantern welcomes spirits and an apple buried in the yard feeds them.

Ring a bell or clap three times, then raise your open arms:

I celebrate the dance of life to death to new life and the balance of the cosmos in my life! The last harvest is gathered and stored for the dark months ahead, and the Wheel of the Year has turned to the time of the Hunter.

Ring a bell or clap nine times:

At this time is the veil between the worlds thin, and I welcome the spirits who have gone before and the Others, who pass between two worlds. This is the Crone's time and with the Lord of the Shadows, She is the passage from life to life that all must take. They give a refreshing rest in the continuous turning of the Spiral Dance that goes and returns, yet ever moves on. With the Ancient Ones, _____ and _____ , I move with the dance unperturbed. Love gives strength; give to gain.

Hold up the wand:

Great Lady _____ , Fruitful Mother, You have showered me with Your bounty, and in this turning of the seasons, I bid You farewell as you walk now as Crone with _____ , the Lord of the Hunt. I know that within You is yet another fruit waiting to be born, and I will bide patient until the Mother returns.

Set the cauldron on the pentacle and light the black votive inside it with the center candle:

Here is the cauldron of endings and new beginnings. Into this burning flame do I cast my weaknesses and

the habits that keep me from attaining my potential.
By the death of these things will I live a better life.
So Mote It Be!

Burn the parchment in the flame, and when it is reduced to ashes, ring bell or clap nine times to signify completion. Then take the white candle and pass it through the patchouli incense or anoint with patchouli oil, to be saved for lighting the jack-o'-lantern.

With this candle and by its light I welcome you
spirits this Samhain night.

Hold the heather over the altar in your power hand:

I call upon the power of this herb to bless this house
and the spirits that come to visit.

Drop the heather into the cauldron candle:

The air is purified and made pleasant for the spirits
and Others who may call upon me. Blessed Be!

Hold the apple above the altar:

I call upon Thee Lord and Lady, _____ and _____ ,
to bless this fruit to be the food for the dead. Let any
who visit find sustenance in this apple and pass on
refreshed. So Mote It Be!

Proceed to Cakes and Wine, then open the Circle and bury the apple outside.

5

Creating Spells

Spells: Pro-active Prayers of Witchcraft

Using the term "spell" brings to mind various connotations to people, yet the actual process of spell casting is found universally. Spells are the mechanism for initiating changes, and as such they are a form of pro-active prayer. Instead of passively beseeching assistance and hoping for the best, the Witch actively calls for changes, connecting with the needed energies and channeling them to achieve the desired goal. By augmenting personal energy with that of the Earth and the spell ingredients, power is increased and a satisfactory resolution is more likely. Spells are done when there is a need, rather than as a means of dialog with the Divine. Meditations, Esbats, and Sabbats are primary communicative activities in Witchcraft, but spells are for when you want something, want to give the energies a push in the desired direction, and have some objective in mind. Even more so than with prayer, however, a key part of spell casting is knowing, or *kenning*, that the spell will work. This means you have no doubts about the success of the spell any more than you would doubt that the Sun will rise in the morning as it has for billions of years. Spells are not questions or petitions, but statements of energy movement for achieving objectives.

There are three major purposes for creating spells, some of which may be worked together to achieve a goal:

Drawing, or bringing, something to you, such as money, love, or health spells

Repelling, banishing, or exorcising something that is already present, such as with cleansing spells

Containing, deflecting, or reflecting something, such as with protection spells

A drawing spell brings to you something you do not currently have, while the repelling spell sends away something currently present that you do not want. The containing spell has the different facets of holding something in place, keeping something at bay, or confining something. When doing a house protection spell, as an example, you first repel (banish) current negative energies, then draw in (bring) positive energies, and finally contain (hold) those energies in place (perhaps with salt or garlic cloves on the floor inside the doorways and window sills). Another house protection spell, called a Witch's Bottle, is a jar containing pins and broken glass to reflect negative energies and diffuse them randomly. A containment spell may also be used to hold existing negative energies at their source, thus keeping these away from your home. While magic is conducted for a variety of reasons, there is still the primary responsibility of acting in conjunction with a code of ethics, lest the results generate a serious personal psychic and spiritual endangerment. The admonition of "harm none" refers to both the magic worker as well as the object of the magical energy. It is just as harmful to yourself, to your own spirit, to pray for something bad to happen to someone else, as it is to create a spell to affect someone else without that person's consent.

The rhythm of incantations in spell casting is like that of childhood rhymes. This is not supposed to make for great poetry, but is simple, catchy, and to the point. This is one of the Witch's methods of prayer that opens the way through the subconscious mind to connect with the Universal Power. While it is best to prepare for spell casting with formulating your own incantation in advance, you can also go with the flow of the moment—but you have to be focused for this. As a beginner, it would be better for you to create the rhyme prior to spell casting, writing it down on a note card or paper for use in the Circle.

Ending a spell with the "So Mote It Be!" expression gives the spell the added emphasis that what has been wrought *must* be. There is no room for pleading or hoping, only the certain knowledge of *must*. By conducting a spell, you are moving energy with dynamic intent and determination, and the words have power in and of themselves to affirm the magic. "So Mote It Be" (SMIB) is a declaration to the Universe that with the love of the Divine and the aid of the Elementals, a magical event *has* taken place. Do not diminish your empowerment by qualifying your magical work. If you have doubts, then wait until you address those before doing the spell work. Here is where meditation will be helpful for seeking out what it is that makes you hesitant. Magic should be a joyful affirmation of union with Nature and the Cosmos, not a matter of uncertainty and fearfulness that only serves to dilute the energy you have raised.

So Mote It Be is also a statement of affirmation of unity, as when stating your connection with the Elementals in body and strength, breath and creativity, energy and enthusiasm, and blood and emotion. The meaning also extends to expressing that this is simply how it is, that there is connection and there is balance. Just as with praying, the vocal tone is different than a bland or normal speaking voice in spell work, for expressiveness adds to the magical power. Think of it as being in an animated conversation with people whose company you find enjoyable and comfortable.

Use the wording of spells to describe the acts you are performing, while citing the ingredients and their function in the spell.

This helps to focus the energies and keeps you on track. You bless the materials used as you progress through the spell, so that if you are going to put mugwort into a cauldron and add hot water to create a brew for washing a crystal ball, you would state: "I bless thee, mugwort, that thy energies work well for me." As you add the hot water, you would state: "I call upon you, mugwort, to cleanse this crystal ball and aid me in my divinations." Then when the water is cooled, you gently wash the crystal ball: "May this wash of blessed mugwort cleanse and awaken the energies for divination in this crystal ball."

While you can think the words of a spell rather than speak them aloud, there is a magical tradition that spoken words have the power of manifestation. Most cultures believe in the power of words, and include this in their religious texts, so if you are shy about speaking, you should meditate on just why this is. Some people do get distracted because they start to listen to their own voice, but this is a matter of focus and can be overcome by paying attention to what you are doing rather than hearing your own voice. Witchcraft offers self-empowerment, and part of this means being able to confront and overcome your limitations.

The Psychology of Magic

Because time is fluid in Witchcraft, seen as a spiral that may be accessed at any point, it is not difficult to work magic with the future results in mind. The subconscious mind is accessed for magical work, and it is also the place where all the activities of daily life first take place. Because of how the neural transmitters function, and the distance run by nerve impulses, all things known by the conscious mind actually take place earlier and are only remembered consciously. In other words, there is a time lag between an event and a person's cognitive awareness of that event. This is why a person might not realize the bath water is too hot until after being in it a few moments—it just takes a while to reg-ister on the conscious mind. Meanwhile, the subconscious mind is already aware of the temperature. Witches practice opening the communication channel with the subconscious mind, so that in the tub example, a Witch would be aware before stepping into the tub that it is too hot. Most people simply go through life without noticing the discrepancy of time, except when something called *deja vu* ("already seen") occurs, and then they wonder why a place or event seems so familiar or has happened before. This is a clue that time does indeed spiral and you can dip into it at will.

Since in a deja vu experience you seem to know in advance what will happen, if only for a short time, you can alter that event. What may be somewhat amusing is the reaction of other people involved in the event. Since they are not connectively using their subconscious mind and not aware as quickly as your-self, you may find they want to react to something that has not happened, giving them a puzzled pause. As an example, I once averted a disastrous dinner argument by keeping silent during the experience when I knew that I was "supposed" to make an inno-cent remark, which led to a fight the first time around. When the time came for my remark, I did not make it and the conversation at the table stopped cold, with everyone turning to look at me! But I had changed history and the table chat resumed without the argument.

When you start altering the future, you may start having multi-ple deja vus of the same event or experience. The meaning of this is that you ran the course of the event, did not like how things turned out, changed it, ran the course again, and still did not like the results, so you are giving it another try or realigning the events prior to the deja vu to make the results more satisfactory. Another aspect, which you will begin to recognize with experience, is that there is a variation in the deja vu from what you knew it once was. That means your prior change has worked, and you are given a second chance with the new arrangement. This facet of time manipulation is characteristic of the Witch's development of subconscious awareness. Witches are people who have refined their ability to process precognitive stimuli and hold on to it so they are able to then alter events before these events register on the conscious minds of other people.

The fluidity of time makes it possible for you to manipulate it so that you can stretch it out, making certain you are never late to any destination. When you are working magic, the conscious mind is silenced or relaxed so the subconscious mind may come forward as the active principle. Doing drumming, breath work, chanting, and dancing during the raising of energy when in the Circle is a way to move yourself into an altered state. Drugs and alcohol are not good for this since these inhibit your awareness. When working magic, the subconscious mind creates the reality, which will then be perceived by the conscious mind.

To be a Witch, you have to be ready to live in multiple layers of reality with multiple worlds (physical, astral, psychic, spiritual, etc.) since these are what you access when practicing your Craft. These worlds exist and are approached with meditation, astral projection, out of body experience, visits to Otherworld or Underworld, pathworking, and spell casting. In the ritual of casting the Circle, you create a space not only to hold the energy you raise, but one that is apart from the rest of the physical world. When you draw the cosmic lemniscate (∞) over the altar, and say that you are standing between the worlds, you say you are "in a place that is not a place, and in a time that is not a time," as a reminder for the subconscious mind to be open. You stand at the nexus of other worlds, where the magic you conduct may travel to affect your physical world.

Types of Spells

In the sense that all things are connected through energy, there are many who feel that all Witchcraft utilizes sympathetic magic. This means that the magic is performed through making correlations between two separate objects so that what happens to one happens to the other, or has an effect on the other. If the magic utilizes something that has been in contact with another physical object of the spell, this is called *contagion magic*, meaning that the energy of the physical object is transferred into the spell. An example of contagion magic might be wrapping a protection amulet in the handkerchief belonging to the person for whom the charm is meant. If only correlations between objects are used, then it is called *homeopathic magic*. An example of this is burning a green candle to draw money to you or to get a pay raise at work, because green is equated to money or growth, and burning the candle releases the energy on your behalf.

The term *sympathetic magic* may be more precisely defined as meaning that one object is visualized as *being* another object, hence what happens to the one happens to the other because they are both the same. Correlations or energy-connected material may be used, or simple visualization may be used. The use of poppets is a familiar example of sympathetic magic—one that goes back to prehistoric times with cave paintings of successful hunts and clay fertility sculptures of pregnant women. By altering the focus to establish a relationship or draw a connection between the spell materials and the focus of the spell, it becomes *comparative magic*, meaning that the spell items *represent* the desired effect or the object of the spell. An example of this is in the Ostara ritual where a seed is planted to represent something you want to sprout in your life. The word "as" in a spell incantation is a clue that it uses comparative magic: "As this green candle burns, money flows to me." You know these are two different things, candle and money, but you compare what happens to the one with what will happen to the other. Another example is when burning incense to cleanse an area: "As this incense smolders, this area is purified."

Simply by changing the focus when using incense for a cleansing, this can become *directive magic*, showing that one thing *affects* another. Now when the incense smoke is wafted in the room, the words used are: "The smoke of this incense cleanses this room of all negative energies." This is one of the most common types of magic in Witchcraft, especially when herbs, crystals, or stones are added to a candle flame. Additionally, the energy qualities of the additives to spells are directed to the spell purpose through directive magic with as little as a simple statement: "Bergamot for wealth."

The last type of spell is *transference* magic, meaning that the energy of one object *enters* into another. This is typical of charms and talismans of protection when these absorb the negative energies in a location. Blessing and then hanging up a braid of garlic bulbs or onions in the kitchen is an old-fashioned transference magic tradition for absorbing negative energies in the home. You do not cook with this braid, but dispose of it with a blessing after a year. Garlic bulbs will become balloon-like by then, with the garlic cloves shriveled away and the outer skin still looking plump, but actually being papery thin, presumably with the undesired energies held inside. This is one magic where it is generally accepted that the movement of energy will be harmful to the recipient, so you have to ask the garlics or onions if they want to help. Garlic and onion both have a very high (powerful) energy vibration because of their willingness to give of themselves for others. Another example of this type of magic is taking a plant to a sick person, with the focus that the ailment leave the person and take up residence in the plant, which will wither. The code of ethics of "harm none" is a reminder to ask the plant first if it will help. This can be done at the florist shop or flower section of the supermarket, and take only the one that you feel is extending its agreement. This is where you have to use your intuition and psychic ability to feel what is being told to you. Part of being a Witch is being able to sense and communicate with plants and animals, else how would you know what leaf an herb is offering to you for your spell work? Without the consent of the recipient in transference magic, you will suffer severe physical, psychic, and spiritual repercussions, even to drawing the transferred energy directly into yourself and failure to succeed with the intended magic.

Conducting Spells

Working magic is somewhat like cooking a new dish. You create your recipe from the ingredients available, matching colors, materials, inscriptions, timing, etc. to match the purpose and focus of the spell. The spell can be as simple or as complex as you want it to be. The way you draw all these elements together is through a list of correspondences you create in your personal Book of Shadows. You perform the spell on the best day, hour, and lunar phase; then see the spell as completed and successful. This means you put it out of your mind unless you are doing a spell that is specifically meant to be drawn out over a period of time, as with a seven-day candle spell. Once the spell work is finished, the materials are disposed of as being energy depleted, or buried to let the energy spread, or placed where the energy is intended to be diffused, as with a protection charm in the glove compartment of your car.

The steps for conducting magic in a ritual format should be noted in your Book of Shadows (BOS), then followed as closely as possible. By using a routine consistently, you are conditioning your subconscious mind, as well as your conscious mind, that something special is about to happen, and so the energy will flow more smoothly. On the following page is a suggested list of steps to add to your BOS.

1. Choose the timing of the spell

2. Outline the ritual and prepare the tools and materials

3. Purify yourself; ground and center

4. Purify the working space (preparing for circle casting)

    a. Light altar candles and incense

    b. Sweep the circle area

5. Cast the circle

    a. Invoke light and the Elemental essence at the Quarters

    b. Draw the energy boundary of the circle

    c. Asperge

    d. Cense

    e. Anoint self

    f. Invoke the Elementals

6. Invoke the Divine (optional)

7. Perform the spell or ritual observance

8. Raise and direct energy

9. Ground the residual power

10. Take some refreshment (may do after opening the circle)

11. Benediction to the Divine (optional)

12. Open the circle

    a. Farewell the Elementals

    b. Snuff the candles at the Quarters (if used)

    c. Withdraw the energy boundary of the circle back into yourself

    d. Balance the energy and ground the excess

Timing enhances the energy and determines the focus for most spell work. The primary factor in Witchcraft for determining spell construction is the phase of the Moon. Any phase except the Dark Moon can be used for spells, as long as the envisionment and focus of the spell is aligned with the lunar energy. Just as the phases of the Moon affect the ocean tides, they are thought to affect the flow of internal fluids, emotions, and energy, so you have to work with the Moon, not contrary to the Moon. As the Moon moves from one sign to another, there is a period called the "Void of Course (VC)," lasting a couple of hours. The VC is usually listed in almanacs, astrological calendars, and many of the annuals by Llewellyn Publications such as the *Magical Almanac*, the *Witches' Datebook*, the *Witches' Calendar*, and the *Astrological Calendar*. The rule of thumb in magic is to avoid the Void, as this time period nullifies energy movement.

The Waxing Moon of the Maiden ☽ begins as the thin sliver of crescent appearing after the Dark Moon and increasing in size until the Moon reaches Full. This Moon phase is favorable for spells of growth, new projects, increase, new beginnings, and drawing desired things to you. This is when you do spells for gaining such things as wealth, happiness, a new job, and love.

The Full Moon of the Mother ◯ is a familiar symbol of Witchcraft, being the most celebrated Esbat and offering the most opportune time for spell work for completions, healing, empowerment, and seeing a goal as fully energized and an accomplished fact. Often a spell might start a few days before the Full Moon so that by ritually moving a candle or burning it an hour each day until the Full Moon, you see the magic as in progress until the final day on which you celebrate attainment of the desired goal. This Moon phase is also good for Rites of Passage such as a Self-Initiation and a Self-Dedication, and it is the time when the Moon can be drawn down into a container of water for charging to use in ritual and magic. It is also when the Goddess energy may be drawn into yourself for prophecy and learning.

The Waning Moon of the Crone ☾ begins as the diminishing size of the Moon after it has been Full, and continues until the Dark Moon. When there is only a thin sliver of the Moon visible prior to becoming totally dark, it is the best time for magical work involving cleansings, releasings, and banishings. This is when you get rid of bad habits or banish poverty, for example. The Dark Moon of the Goddess as Crone or Mystery ● is a good time for divinations and spiritual meditations.

As you plan your magical work, you select the components of the spell from your list of correspondences according to the correlations of the topics (herbs, colors, days, hours, etc.), and according to the structure of the spell (charm, candle burning, sachet, poppet, potpourri, knot tying, etc.). It is more effective to have a single word image in mind to state emphatically at the height of energy raising so it is released and sent out quickly to perform the purpose of the spell. When gathering your spell ingredients from Nature, or purchasing them at a store, the exchange of a gift or of money creates an exchange of energy binding or connecting the spell materials to be directed to accomplish your goals during spell casting. There are any number of formats you can follow for the spell event, but here is a sample format you can work from to prepare your magical experience:

1. Decide what you want to accomplish and how you want to do this (purpose and type of spell)

2. Decide what tools you will need (wand, athame, cauldron, pentacle, crystals, etc.)

3. Decide how you want to manifest the goal (candle burning, knotting, poppet, herbal potpourri, charm, sachet, etc.)

4. Decide what materials you will need (candles, herbs, stones, cloth, oils, shells, feathers, paper, containers, etc.)

5. Decide when the spell will take place (lunar phase, day, hour)

6. Decide what words will be used in the ritual and how the energy will be raised (chanting, dancing, drumming, etc.)

Planning your spells ahead helps to ensure you have the right materials on hand and that you are working during the most advantageous time. One way to decide when to conduct a spell is with the planetary association for the days of the week and for the hours of the day. If your goal is to draw money, you look at the planets influencing money, then perform your spell on a day and at an hour influenced by that planet. Here are the correspondences for the planets, the energies they affect, and what days they most influence.

Planetary Associations

Sun: ☉ Sunday—individuality, pride, success, honors, energy, display, hope, fortune, money, work, power, healing, promotions, strength, spirituality; associated with the number 1 and the colors gold, orange, white, and yellow

Moon: ☾ Monday—dreams, emotions, clairvoyance, home, family, medicine, personality, intuition, cycles, sensitivity, peace, theft, merchandising; associated with the number 2 and the colors silver, white, and gray

Mars: ♂ Tuesday—dynamic energy, aggressiveness, willpower, sex drive, war, matrimony, enemies, prison, hunting, surgery, courage, politics, contests; associated with the number 9 and the colors red and orange

Mercury: ☿ Wednesday—communication, skill, agility, thinking, sensory, learning, teaching, reason, divination, debt, fear, self-improvement, loss; associated with the number 5 and the colors yellow, violet, and iridescent

Jupiter: ♃ Thursday—health, honor, luck, wealth, clothing, money, optimism, opportunity, legal matters, desires, expansion, financial matters, wealth, idealism, justice; associated with the number 3 and the colors blue, indigo, purple, and violet

Venus: ♀ Friday—sociability, friendships, emotions, artistry, values, luxury, love, social activities, strangers, pleasure, art, music, fragrances; associated with the number 6 and the colors pink, green, and aqua

Saturn: ♄ Saturday—ambition, structure, realism, self-preservation, business, self-control, restrictions, freedom, materiality, self-discipline, life, building, doctrine, protection, the elderly, destroying diseases and pests; associated with the number 8 and the colors black, dark gray, and indigo

The rest of the planets do not have daily or hourly associations, but they do have magical associations that may be envisioned for accessing their energies through drawing their symbols on spell material, and using the numbers or colors associated with them. By etching the planetary symbol on a candle or piece of paper, verbally addressing the energy of that planet, you draw that power into your work. Burning the candle so the symbol is melted, or burning the paper with your incantation and planetary symbol on it, releases the energy into action. Here are the symbols and correlations for the other planets:

Neptune: ♆ —occultism, subconscious, psychic energy, spirit, Otherworld, idealism, creativity, illusion; associated with the number 7 and the colors purple and lavender

Uranus: ♅ —sudden and unpredictable changes, tensions, news, originality, knowledge, innovation, divination; associated with the number 4 and the colors green and variegated (colors mixed together, as with a rainbow candle)

Pluto: ♇ —rebirth, transformation, sex, death, spirituality, extremes, evolution, life cycle free from bondage, Underworld; associated with the 0 and the colors brown and black

For timing by hourly influences, the twenty-four-hour day is divided into twelve hours of daytime and twelve hours of nighttime, but for spell work, the timing should be selected by the ac-

Planetary Hours for Day and Night

Sunrise Hours

Hour	Sun.	Mon.	Tues.	Wed.	Thurs.	Fri.	Sat.
1	Sun	Moon	Mars	Mercury	Jupiter	Venus	Saturn
2	Venus	Saturn	Sun	Moon	Mars	Mercury	Jupiter
3	Mercury	Jupiter	Venus	Saturn	Sun	Moon	Mars
4	Moon	Mars	Mercury	Jupiter	Venus	Saturn	Sun
5	Saturn	Sun	Moon	Mars	Mercury	Jupiter	Venus
6	Jupiter	Venus	Saturn	Sun	Moon	Mars	Mercury
7	Mars	Mercury	Jupiter	Venus	Saturn	Sun	Jupiter
8	Sun	Moon	Mars	Mercury	Jupiter	Venus	Saturn
9	Venus	Saturn	Sun	Moon	Mars	Mercury	Jupiter
10	Mercury	Jupiter	Venus	Saturn	Sun	Moon	Mars
11	Moon	Mars	Mercury	Jupiter	Venus	Saturn	Sun
12	Saturn	Sun	Moon	Mars	Mercury	Jupiter	Venus

Sunset Hours

Hour	Sun.	Mon.	Tues.	Wed.	Thurs.	Fri.	Sat.
1	Jupiter	Venus	Saturn	Sun	Moon	Mars	Mercury
2	Mars	Mercury	Jupiter	Venus	Saturn	Sun	Jupiter
3	Sun	Moon	Mars	Mercury	Jupiter	Venus	Saturn
4	Venus	Saturn	Sun	Moon	Mars	Mercury	Jupiter
5	Mercury	Jupiter	Venus	Saturn	Sun	Moon	Mars
6	Moon	Mars	Mercury	Jupiter	Venus	Saturn	Sun
7	Saturn	Sun	Moon	Mars	Mercury	Jupiter	Venus
8	Jupiter	Venus	Saturn	Sun	Moon	Mars	Mercury
9	Mars	Mercury	Jupiter	Venus	Saturn	Sun	Jupiter
10	Sun	Moon	Mars	Mercury	Jupiter	Venus	Saturn
11	Venus	Saturn	Sun	Moon	Mars	Mercury	Jupiter
12	Mercury	Jupiter	Venus	Saturn	Sun	Moon	Mars

tual hour of sunrise or sunset. This means that if the Sun rises on Monday at 7 A.M., then the first hour of sunrise is 7 to 8 A.M. and it is influenced by the Moon. The rest of the hours follow according to the chart until the actual hour of sunset. If the Sun sets at 8:45 P.M., then the first hour from 8:45 P.M. to 9:45 P.M. is influenced by Venus, and the rest of the sunset hours follow in sequence as on the chart. The time for sunrise and sunset is usually in the daily newspaper, as well as on the TV weather channel and in almanacs. By looking at the chart, you can select the hour of the day most convenient for you for performing spells. If you want to do a spell for money, you could use the day of Jupiter (Thursday) and the hour of Jupiter (the first or eighth hour of sunrise, or the third or tenth hour of sunset). This brings the maximum planetary influence for increase of wealth, dealing with financial matters, or gaining luck for drawing money. (See the chart on page 125 for correspondences for timing.)

A talisman is something that you make and carry with you or wear for protection or to attract a particular energy. A crystal, gem, or stone may be made into a talisman by inscribing or painting it with a symbol that represents your intention, be it protection, safe travel, or business success. It is then carried or placed where you want it to have the best effect. You should reinvigorate the talisman periodically by placing it in the light of the Full Moon, or passing it through the symbols of the Elementals during an Esbat celebration. Talismans are often made from metal and have a design relating to the focus of the piece, be it to represent a religious or spiritual approach, draw positive energies into your life, or enhance personal or career ambitions. The symbols may be designs of protection such as ⍟ or ⊠ , or *bindrunes* created from combining two to three runic letters with the last one being the one that binds it. Meanings for the runic alphabet are given later in this chapter.

An amulet is usually a natural item that attracts energies, such as carrying a four-leaf clover for good luck and money. The effectiveness of the amulet is related to the perceived energy of the object. Various objects are traditionally considered magical, including a rabbit's foot or a chicken's foot, feathers, acorns, roots such as fennel or mandrake, and palm fronds. Crystals, stones, and gems may work as amulets as well, if not worn as adornment but for their energy properties. These, too, may have inscriptions added to them, and thus a painted or inscribed stone may blur the line between amulet and talisman while nevertheless providing magical energy. Normally, amulets are not intended as adornment, but are worn or carried for their energy properties.

To charge the amulet or talisman requires a focus on what it is supposed to do for you. If you see the object as attracting success, as attracting good luck, then you will want to use the Waxing up to the Full Moon. But if you intend the object to deflect, repel, or return-to-sender negative energies, you will want to charge it by the Waning up to, but not including, the Dark Moon.

Spells are generally done for the personal growth and happiness of the individual Witch, but sometimes people will ask for spells. This is difficult since the person must be fully in accord with the process or the spell energy will be muted or even misdirected. It would be better to avoid doing spells for others until you are proficient at working spells for yourself. Then, you may consider whether you want to do magic for others, what ethical considerations are involved with what the person desires you to do, what gift you should receive in payment, be it money or barter, and what the real facts in a matter are. You need to maintain your ethical standard and preserve yourself from unwanted negative energies or Karmic backlash.

If the spell cast does not seem to work, you may need to reexamine the timing and the goal. Was the Moon in the Void of Course? Was the planetary day or hour inappropriate? Were you acting within the ethical guidelines of the Rede? Were you attempting to evade a life lesson you need to learn? Try meditating on where the spell was inadequate, and listen to what comes to you. Sometimes people subvert their own workings, either because they really do not believe they can make a change, or because they haphazardly threw together ingredients without a clear understanding of what energies they wanted to work with. When a spell does not work, it is usually because of one of these reasons, and refocusing may help you overcome the obstacles to cast a more appropriate spell.

Using Lists of Correspondences

While there will be numerous entries in your Book of Shadows relating to such things as your personal philosophy, a code of ethics, Esbat and Sabbat Rituals, Circle Casting and Opening, tools and alphabets, the most important and most frequently used things will be your lists of correspondences for spells. You decide what lists you need and what you want on them, and your lists will help to make your magical practice consistent. Not everyone sees the same correlations in magical usage, and so you may alter these as inclined by your intuition, but there are a number of traditionally accepted correspondences that are generally recognized among practitioners of the Craft. If you have the time to gather as much like-energy together for a spell, then matching the days, colors, herbs, and hours will give you a sense of structure and solidity you may require for optimal focusing. The fact that so many magic workers utilize the same images increases the correlation of these images in the astral realm, from which then the manifestations can be drawn.

The lists for the lunar phases, days of the week, planetary influences, and hours of the day have already been provided, but another important correlation is that of color. These are important in the construction of spell work for their energy vibration and subconscious effect on your mind. If you have other associations for these colors, add them to your list, then use these for selecting the cloths for charm bags, or in choosing the color of your working candle. The colors help to further align the desired energies for the spell being constructed.

Color Correspondences

Amber: energizing, empowerment, Witchcraft skills

Black: protection, truth, ward negativity, spirit contact, binding spell work

Blue (dark): truth, dreams, protection, change, meditation, impulse

Blues (light): health, psychic awareness, intuition, opportunity, understanding, quests, safe journey, patience, tranquillity, ward depression

Brown: earthly riches, endurance, influence, houses/homes, animal health, steadiness, physical objects, grounding, gaining special favors

Copper: money/business/professional increase, career/energy maneuvers

Gold: success, wealth, achievement, power, healing, mental/physical strength, divination, intuition, safety, happiness, playfulness

Gray: veiling, neutralizing, vision quests, Otherworld

Green: money, prosperity, fertility, employment, healing, luck, the Wildwood, Nature magic, balance, courage, agriculture, changing direction/attitudes

Indigo: spiritual growth, meditation, spirit communication, learn ancient wisdom

Lavender: spiritual development, psychic growth, divination, Otherworld

Orange: strength, action, healing, mental clarity, vitality, attracting things, luck, success, career, dominance, ambition, property, justice, legal matters, encouragement, adaptability, sales, business deals

Pink: love, romance, partnership, affection, nurturing, peace, honor, morality, friendships, sociability, good will, caring, healing emotions

Purple: protection, self-assurance, power, intuition, wisdom, occultism, spiritual development, spirit communication, progress, ambition, healing, progress, business, influencing higher-ups

Rainbow: variegate colors, inner development by relaxation, meditation, and introspection

Red: power, vitality, strength, energy, health, enthusiasm, courage, passion, drive, sexuality, survival, victory

Silver: psychic development, meditation, astral energies, success, balance, ward negativity

Violet: self-improvement, intuition, success in searches

White: protection, truth, purity, meditation, peace, sincerity, justice, ward doubts

Yellow: divination, clairvoyance, creativity, mental alertness, intellect, memory, learning, self-promotion, harmony, prosperity, changes

Herbs add energy and potency to spells through their inherent qualities and through their overall association with the Elementals: Earth with their roots, leaves, flowers, nuts, and berries; Air with their fragrance and pollens; Fire with their growth from sunlight and their internally affecting qualities; and Water in their growth, juices, and nourishment. While some herbs are common household spices used in cooking, and their magical qualities may be called upon during cooking as well as for incenses and when making charms or doing candle spells, you should never take herbs internally unless you are absolutely certain they are not harmful. You may add leaves, roots, bark, twigs, berries, and nuts to spell work according to the correlations and the type of spell you are creating. You can buy herbs in health stores, occult supply stores, grocery stores, and as herbal teas. Call upon the energies of dried herbs as you release them into action through dropping into a candle flame, or by placing them in a pouch and passing it through the symbols of the Elementals. When using these lists, you look at what has the desired influence, and what you actually have on hand to work with. You could end up reworking a spell to make use of available materials. Pick only one or two of the herbs for use, not all of them listed under a category. Here is a simple list of herbs, trees, and shrubs intended for magical use only:

Herbal/Plant Listing by Uses

Balance: basil, chamomile, mullein, nettle, woodruff

Blessing: chamomile, dianthus, elderflower, fennel, mint, oat, rosemary, vervain

Cleansing/Purification: betony, burdock, clove, hyssop, lavender, mullein, parsley, pine, rosemary, thyme, vervain, yarrow

Consecration: acacia, anise seed, basil, clover, hyssop, lavender, mugwort, nettle, rosemary, sunflower, vervain

Countering Negative Energies: agrimony, fennel, hyssop, motherwort, vervain

Courage: basil, borage, mullein, rosemary, thyme

Creativity: anise seed, basil, catnip, hawthorn, lavender, St. Johnswort, vervain

Divination: anise seed, basil, bay, cinquefoil, clover, damiana, dittany of Crete, eyebright, honeysuckle, hops, lavender, marigold, moonwort, mugwort, mullein, orange peel, thyme, vervain, woodruff, yarrow

Encourage Change: linden, purple heather, woodruff

Energy/Power/Strength: cinquefoil, elder flower, fennel, St. Johnswort, vervain, woodruff

Fortune/Justice: bay, bergamot, cinquefoil, lemon balm, orange peel, star anise, vervain, woodruff

Happiness/Peace: fennel, lavender, loosestrife, rosemary, vervain, yarrow

Healing: cinquefoil, comfrey, coriander, hops, lavender, lemon balm, mullein, mustard, rosemary, sage, St. Johnswort, tansy, thyme

Love: apple, basil, cardamom, catnip, dill flowers, elm, ginger, lavender, lemonbalm, linden leaves, marigold, marjoram, moonwort, mustard seed, orange peel, red heather, rosemary, vetivert, yarrow

Meditation: acacia, benzoin, chamomile, woodruff

Money: basil, bergamot, chamomile, clove, dill seeds, mint, moonwort, nutmeg, oat, vetivert

Protection/Defense: betony, birch, burdock, cumin, dianthus, dill leaves, fennel, fern, marjoram, mint, mugwort, mullein, mustard, parsley, rosemary, sage, vervain, white heather, woodruff, yarrow

Psychic Awareness: bay, betony, burdock, cinnamon, elderflower, lavender, mace, marigold, star anise, woodruff

Releasing Negativity: betony, clove, hyssop, mugwort, rosemary, St. Johnswort, thyme, vervain, vetivert, yarrow

Sealing/Sending Positive Energy: angelica, cinquefoil

Spirit Contact/Blessings: lilac, purple heather, mint, Solomon's seal

Strength/Willpower: rosemary, St. Johnswort

Wisdom: elder, sage, willow

Incenses add their energies to your work and increase your focus on the desired results from spell work. They also create a suitable atmosphere for meditation, divination, and other spiritual activities. Incense may be burned to enhance spell work or an appropriate ritual, some coming as premade sticks, cones, or bundles, and others as loose herbs or resins burned in candles or on charcoal disks. If using the disks, be sure to have proper ventilation since the charcoal consumes oxygen, and could lead to suffocation in a closed area. Smudging is when an herbal bundle is burned so the smoke will affect an area, such as a room being used as the magical space, or preparing a space for ritual or meditation. The following is a list of incenses according to their uses.

Incense Listed by Uses

Anointing: frankincense, jasmine, lavender, rose, vervain, orange

Balance: cypress, jasmine, sandalwood, sweetgrass

Banishing or Releasing: clove, cypress, mugwort, sage, lemon, lime

Binding: cypress, dragon's blood, rowan, vetivert

Blessing or Consecration: copal, frankincense, rosemary, sweetgrass

Changes: bayberry, dragon's blood, lilac, patchouli, woodruff

Divination or Clairvoyance: bay, copal, lilac, mugwort, myrrh, sage

Cleansing: cedar, frankincense, lavender, pine, sage, sandalwood

Consecration: benzoin, copal, frankincense, lavender, myrrh, sandalwood

Creativity: dragon's blood, lavender, orange, rosemary, savory, tangerine

Courage: cinnamon, dragon's blood, patchouli, rosemary

Cursing: bayberry, clove, dragon's blood, myrrh

Exorcism: copal, bayberry, frankincense, lavender, mullein, rosemary, sage

Gain Goals: acacia, bay, cedar, cinnamon, dragon's blood, orange, sandalwood

Luck or Justice: bay, bayberry, jasmine, patchouli, sandalwood, violet

Happiness or Peace: jasmine, lavender, orange, rose, vervain, sandalwood

Inspiration or Wisdom: acacia, copal, frankincense, oak moss, pine, sage

Love: cinquefoil, jasmine, lavender, mugwort, orange, rose

Meditation: acacia, copal, cypress, cedar, frankincense, jasmine, sage

Power/Strength: dragon's blood, frankincense, patchouli, verbena

Protection or Defense: bayberry, frankincense, myrrh, jasmine, rosemary

Psychic Centers: basil, bay, copal, frankincense, lavender, mugwort, woodruff

Reincarnation: basil, lilac, patchouli, rose, sandalwood, sweetgrass

Visions: basil, bay, copal, frankincense, mugwort, sage

Willpower: bay, cedar, dragon's blood, patchouli, rosemary, sage, woodruff

Incenses Used as Smudges

Cedar: calm, comfort, purification, protection

Juniper: centering, clarity, cleansing, focus

Lemongrass: refreshing, communications, channeling

Pine: cleansing, renewal, strengthening

Sage: cleansing, balance, banish negativity, strengthening

Sweetgrass: ancient wisdom, call to ancestors, call for spirit helpers

Just as incenses are derived from a number of the herbs, flowers, roots, and nuts listed, so are essential oils. You can therefore select for your spells the herbs you want, then match the incense and essential oils accordingly. The practice of the Craft is rather like selecting choices from a menu of options. There are herbs that can be burned in a candle, stuffed into a dream pillow, added to an object, rubbed on to a tool or spell item, or sewn up into a charm; there are incenses to enhance the atmosphere for the intended purpose of the Craft work; and there are essential oils to dress candles, tools, and objects energizing them according to the properties of the herbs from which they are derived. Oils can also be used to consecrate the altar and the Witch during rituals, and while most any oil may be used, benzoin or rose are typical, while cinnamon will burn the skin. The following is a sample listing.

Essential Oils

Bay: attain desires; success; clarity of visions or dreams

Basil: intuition; optimism; psychic awareness

Cedar: cleansing; strength; meditation

Cinnamon: energy; courage, gain goals, gain money

Citrus Lemon/Lime: invigorate; joy; energy

Cypress: calmative; soothes emotions; stability; Underworld

Frankincense: cleanse aura; enhance psychic power; energizer

Jasmine: love; intuition; spirituality; confidence; sexuality

Lavender: balance; calming; cleansing; exorcism; Otherworld

Orange: visions; psychic dreams; restfulness

Patchouli: Earth energy; sexuality; strength; power; Underworld

Peppermint: alertness; action; mental clarity

Pine: energy; cleansing, strength, clarity, action; protection

Rose: energy; love; gentleness; peace; happiness

Rosemary: mental clarity; memory; protection; invigorate; blessing

Sage: purify; cleanse; spiritual visions; inspiration

Sandalwood: cleanse; purify; energy

Vetivert: internal alignment; unified energies

When composing your spell, you may want to add the power of sigils and symbols, and there are special meanings associated with the runes. Not only are these letters of the alphabet, but the letters themselves have an energy influence. While you may inscribe a candle or a talisman with some of the planetary symbols already shown, you could further enhance the spell with runic symbols. When using runes, you could coordinate the color associated with the rune with the color of the object you are placing it on, such as a stone or crystal as with a talisman. Here is a list of these meanings:

Runic Symbols

Name	Sign	Letter	Meaning	Color
Osa	F	[OE]	the God; good fortune; favorable outcome	green/white
As	ᚪ	[AE]	ancestor; signs; gain ancient wisdom	indigo/purple
Beorc	ᛒ	[B]	Goddess; fertility; growth; beginnings	white/green
Daeg	ᛞ	[D]	daybreak; between the worlds; breakthrough	pale violet
Eh	ᛖ	[E]	movement; safe journey; progress; changes	blue
Feoh	ᚠ	[F]	material wealth; fulfillment; ambition satisfied	green
Gefu	ᚷ	[G]	union; partnership; love; gifts; self-confidence	pink/red

Name	Sign	Letter	Meaning	Color
Eoh	ᛇ	[Z]	a channel; action; Otherworld communication	indigo/purple
Haegl	ᚻ	[H]	hail; limits/disruptions; awakening	white/blue
Is	ᛁ	[I]	ice; immobility; rest period; stop slander	white/silver
Gera	ᛃ	[J]	year; harvest; rewards; actual results from work	white/green
Ken	ᚲ	[K/C]	transforming fire; opening energy; fresh start	white/gold
Lagu	ᛚ	[L]	fluidity; water; psychic power; intuition; vitality	blue/violet
Mannaz	ᛗ	[M]	Self; self-improvement; cooperation; meditation	indigo/violet
Nyd	ᚾ	[N]	constraint; self-control; conquer obstacles	white/blue
Ing	ᛝ	[NG]	the Horned God; fertility; family; completion	indigo
Ethel	ᛟ	[OE]	possession; home; social status; acquisitions	white/gold
Perth	ᛈ	[P]	destiny; hidden forces; sudden luck; initiation	blue/green
Rad	ᚱ	[R]	travel; quest; find what is sought; attunement	blue/violet
Sigel	ᛋ	[S/Z]	wholeness; healing; energy; power	orange/gold/red
Tyr	ᛏ	[T]	victory; success; courage; favorable outcome	white/gold
Thorn	ᚦ	[TH]	protection; gateway; foes neutralized; defense	black
Uruz	ᚢ	[U]	strength; physical health; courage; promotion	green/brown

Name	Sign	Letter	Meaning	Color
Wyn	ᚹ	[W]	joy; comfort; happiness; harmony; love	pink/yellow
Eolh	ᚦ	[EA]	elk; protection; friendship; going unnoticed	white
Wyrd	[ ]	[—]	unknowable fate; destiny; cosmic influence	black/white

Basic Spell Runes and Symbols

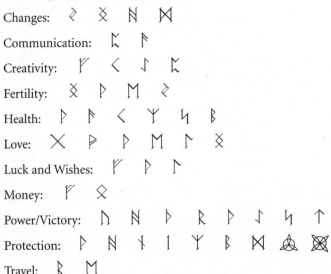

Changes:

Communication:

Creativity:

Fertility:

Health:

Love:

Luck and Wishes:

Money:

Power/Victory:

Protection:

Travel:

Magical Practice

Working spells with candles is one of the most common and effective magical practices, but this requires taking some precau-
tions to avoid burns or fires. Remove the paper sticker from the
bottom of votive candles, and always be sure the container you are
using will hold the melted wax without breaking, spillage, or creating a fire hazard. If burning a votive candle in a glass container
provided for that purpose, *never* hold the glass once the candle is
melted because it is extremely hot and you do not want to burn

your fingers or drop the glass, spreading burning wax. The best container for candle spells in which herbs will be dropped into the candle flame is a metal cauldron with feet (usually three), which you should set on a tile or other material to avoid scorching the surface of your altar. The average working cauldron is between six and twelve inches across the top, and three to six inches deep. Anything smaller could be a problem for holding melted wax. A layer of clean sand on the bottom of the cauldron will help to stabilize the candle. To clean, boil some water and place your cauldron in a larger pot, then pour the hot water into the pot so it is outside the cauldron. Wait a few minutes, and the internal wax ought to loosen enough to be popped out with a paper towel for disposal. Using a pottery cauldron could result in heat breakage and the seepage of hot wax through the bottom. Remember that oils will burn, so do not pour oil into a burning candle. Dressing a candle does not require a lot of oil, and it is done before the candle is lit; nevertheless this is another reason for placing the candle in a secure container. While you are working the candle, putting on the oils and symbols, you state what you are doing and why, maintaining your focus on the desired effect and visualizing it. See the power going into the candle as you put on the oil, see the effect occurring as you inscribe the candle, and by the end of the spell, you will envision the effect as done.

As you add herbs to the flame, feel the herbal energies moving into the spell. See the energies build in power, which you can aid at this point with dance, chant, and gesture, and when you feel the energy level is at the highest you can tolerate, release the energies by directing them to their purpose. Remember to use a short phrase or key word to send the power out to complete the spell. As soon as you send that energy to complete the task, see the spell as completed with the desired effect as attained.

Let the candle burn for an hour on the altar. That is all that is needed, but if you are feeling a sense of completion energy you may want to let it burn longer. If you are doing spell work in conjunction with an Esbat, you could let the candle continue to burn as you complete that ritual, take some refreshment, ground (earth) the excess energy, open your circle, and put away your tools—except for the candle on the altar. Once the hour of candle burning is over (or a longer time if you feel the need), you may snuff out the candle, looking at any floating debris or images forming in the cooling wax for interpretation. Record what you saw, perhaps drawing a little sketch for later reference, then dispose of the remaining used candle by burying it in earth, placing it in the garbage to go into a landfill, or tossing it into moving water. When doing these spells with votive candles, there usually is not very much material left, which makes it easier to dispose of the remains.

Besides selecting a candle based on the color, you have the choice of styles. Tapers are good for altars, meditation, and divination. Seven-knobbed candles are good when you want to use one knob per day for a seven-day spell of drawing or repelling. Other candle shapes and styles include cat, dragon, male or female figures, owl, pillar, skull, snake, and votive. The pillar and votive candles can be inscribed with runic symbols and planetary symbols before lighting, and these are easy for dropping in herbs, little stones, or small crystals. The stone and crystals could also be arranged around the base of the candle or container. Skull candles are good for spells dealing with creativity, divination, dreams, memory, mental clarity, and spirit or Otherworld communication. Cat candles are used for spells for animals, cleverness, enlightenment, power, luck, protection, contacting spirit guides, and warding negativity. Figurine candles can be used in spells dealing with personal matters such as business success, health, energy, promotion, love, peace, ritual purification, and fertility. Owls and snakes are associated with wisdom, clear-sightedness, astral travel, longevity, spiritual development, and shedding the past, while dragons are symbolic of power, defense, stability, strength, and energy.

Outlining your spell will help you put together the necessary ingredients before you begin your magical event. Write it out, perform the spell, and then, if using a candle, look for symbols and signs in the melted wax as it cools. With melted candle wax, there may be images present that can offer an interpretation. Using the edge of the container furthest from you on the altar as North and the closest as South, think of these regions as 12:00 and 6:00, for where the image lies may tell you when to expect the results to appear or how the spell will manifest. The East of the container is 3:00 and the West is 9:00, but these can be interpreted as days of the week, or weeks of the month as well. Often the symbols will simply verify to you that the spell has been effective, and not all of the symbols you see will be interpreted according to the listing in the next chapter. You have to use your intuitive powers to interpret the images in the wax, and that is part of what makes Witchcraft an art. Do not feel restricted to the meanings in any list of symbols if your instinct is telling you something else. With all your spells, note what happened as a result of the spell.

When sewing poppets or herbal pouches, the thread, cloth, and herbs are all coordinated to have the same energy signals. Your focus remains on the desired result of the object, and when finished, you place it where intended. With protection pouches, it is good to renew the energies periodically by placing in the light of the Full Moon, or passing through the symbols of the Elementals. You can infuse more energy into an object by thinking about it, drawing up energy as when grounding and centering, and passing the energy through your hands into the object.

Elixirs may be used as a wash for a ritual or spell object, or may be drunk as an internal energy enhancer. The following list indicates stone energies for elixirs in parentheses. All that is needed to create this drink is spring water and the stone, placed in the water under the light of the Full Moon, and stored, perhaps with a drop of an alcohol such as vodka, whiskey, rum, or gin as a preservative. If you abstain from alcohol, do not use this method of preservation, but instead simply keep the elixir tightly bottled and store in a cool, dark place. Here is a listing of some easy to locate stones:

Magical Stones and Crystals (Elixir Benefits)

Agate: health, good fortune, eloquence, vitality, energy, self-confidence, bursts of mental/physical energy, balance emotions, calm the body, mind, and emotions; *Banded:* relieve stress; *Blue-Lace:* calm, third eye, self-expression, neutralize anger; (encourage trust and friendliness); *White with Blue/Black Spots:* travel; *Eye Formation:* bodily protection, travel; *Mossy:* healing, cleansing, strength, abundance, self-confidence, harmony, release anger or frustration, Earth energies connection; *Milky with Red:* visualization skills, gain goals

Amber: strengthen/break spell—a Witch stone, increase, success, health, healing, love, absorb negative energy, manifestation, good luck; (eases gloom)

Amethyst: spirituality, protection from negativity through transformation, intuition, dreams, relieve tension, meditation, cleansing/energizing, protect against psychic manipulation; (help in compromise)

Apache Tear: protection from directed negative energies, grounding energies, spiritual meditation

Aquamarine: psychological influence, inspire thought process, good luck in tests, positive interviews; (calms; relieves tension)

Aventurine: creativity, luck in physical activities, courage, calm, sleep, leadership, decision-making; (soothe eyes; gain an open mind; curb pride and aloofness)

Azurite (blended blues and greens): psychic development; meditation; facing fears, healing, visions; (help in controlling own reality)

Beryl: intellect, willpower, aid heart and digestive system; (build self-esteem)

Bloodstone (Heliotrope): remove obstacles, vitality, enhance talents, balance, health/healing, ward injury, purify the blood, courage, strength, integrity; (curb obsessive affection)

Boji Stone (paired: one smooth, one bumpy with projections): strengthen chakras, healing, regenerative, balance energy fields

Calcite: Gold: healing, cheerfulness; (reach for new goals or emotional contacts); *Green:* soothe fears, calm, aid intuition, transitions; *Orange:* physical energy, expand awareness, intuition

Carnelian: career success, fast action, shield thoughts, good health, protection, grounding, motivation, personal power

Chrysocolla: balance, cleanse negativity, contentment, healing, prosperity, good luck, clears mind; (open a path away from daily routine)

Chrysoprase: peace, meditation, clairvoyance, gain incentive; (temper egotism)

Citrine: success, clear thinking, protection, direction, induce dreams, improve self-image or self-confidence, prosperity, manifest personal power, initiative, creativity, endurance

Coral: calm, relaxation, protect from illness, ward unwanted thought energies

Emerald: artistic talent, memory, truth, visions, business success, peace, love, psychic insight, tranquillity

Fluorite: meditation, Fairy Realms, dreams, past lives, aids intellect, heals energy drains in the aura, ground, balance, focus energy, absorb or alter negative energy; discernment, aid concentration

Garnet: swift movement, balance energies, revitalization, self-esteem, confidence, dreamwork, energy or courage, love or bonding, devotion

Geodes: freedom of spirit, linking with the cosmic dance

Hematite: communication skills, astral projection, balance and focus energy, clear/calm reasoning, draw good relationships; (lessen defenselessness)

Herkimer Diamond: relieve stress, power booster for crystals/bojis, dream interpretation, psychic attunement; (gain goals, freer expression of love)

Iolite: self-confidence, taking control of your life, self-empowerment

Iron Pyrite: attract success, health, wealth, happiness, intellect, creativity, psychic development, channeling, memory

Jade: peace, cleansing, harmony, friendship, good luck, protection, safe travel, wisdom, long life, dream focus or content; (realistic or practical ideals)

Jasper: strengthen energy flow, relieve stress, gather energy for directing, nurturing, protection, grounding, safe astral travel; *Red:* returns negativity to sender; defensive magics; *Brown:* grounding and stability; soothes nerves; *Green:* healing and fertility

Jet: bind energy to a goal—a Witch stone, calm fears, protection

Lapis Lazuli: authority, power booster, aura cleanser, psychic development, mental balance, self-awareness, inner truths and wisdom, access Universal knowledge

Malachite: business success, protection, vision quest, meditation, prosperity, hope, health, happiness, avert confusion or apathy, manifest desires; (ease focus for controlling reality)

Moldavite (green meteorite glass): transformation, star communication, heal longing, find life purpose, dimensional travel; (decision making, confidence, refocusing)

Moonstone: psychic ability, divination, love, comfort, peace, long life, friends, inspiration, draw attachment/sensitivity, wish granting, new start; (ease in surroundings, curb spending)

Obsidian: Black: protection, scrying, Dark Aspect meditation, Otherworld contact, Shadowland contact, banish grief, benevolence, healing; *Green:* protection of income; open financial opportunities; *Snowflake:* grounding, responsibility, purification, change, growth, deflect negative energy

Onyx: equilibrium, end worry, justice, concentration, devotion, guidance through dreams or meditation, balance of duality; *Black:* deal with emotions or frustration

Petrified Wood: past lives recall, physical energy, preservation of strength, firmness of stance, serenity, balance, grounding, vitality

Pumice: power, manifestation

Quartz Crystal: psychic power, vision quest, protection, energy, divination, projection, attain goals, cleanse aura, meditation, intuition, store and focus energy, or direct and transmit energy; (protection); *Blue:* release emotional tension, soothe; *Rock Crystal:* scrying; energizing; water magics; *Rose:* peace, love, comfort, companionship; (self-discipline, responsibility); *Rutilated:* increase strength of will; (control self-indulgence); *Smoky:* generate energy, protection, purify energies, Fairy connection, disperse negative/draw positive energy; (personal interactions); *Snowy:* meditation, serenity, peace, contemplation

Rhodochrosite: generate energy, physical and emotional balance, heal trauma, union of male and female aspects; (regain emotional energy after frustrations)

Ruby: protect health/wealth, increase energy/creativity, self-confidence, intuition, contentment, courage, spiritual wisdom, generate heat

Ruby Zoisite: leadership, spirituality, aids scholarship, augments teaching skills, boosts public service

Sapphire: wisdom, material gains, attract good influences, peace of mind, hope

Sardonyx: draw troubles, then toss stone into the sea, self-protection

Selenite: calming for meditation/visualization, clarify thoughts, healing; (overcome guilt, let go of negativity, curb overactive fantasizing)

Sodalite: meditation, enhance memory, relieve stress, aid sleep, enhance logical thought, stimulate intellect; (control rage, curb need for negative attention)

Staurolite (Fairy Cross): good luck, protection, security, manifesting higher self on Earth plane, astral connection, confidence.

Sugilite: logic, business expertise, astral travel, manifestation, self-healing

Sunstone: energy, healing, success

Tiger-Eye: Golden Brown: good luck, objectivity, truth, self-confidence, protection from ill will of others, harmony, grounding, stability, instinctive/psychic ability, wisdom, healing; (builds self-confidence); *Green:* good fortune, draws money and stable income

Topaz: Blue: psychic insight, spiritual growth, leadership, concentration, clarity of thought; *Yellow:* stress, deep sleep, psychic ability, calm body and mind, fulfillment of dreams or wishes by focusing into the facets, intentional creation, healing, prosperity, other realms, revitalize bodily energies; (commitment to action, building willpower and decisiveness)

Tourmaline: beauty, freshness, joy, friendship, grounding, protection, calm, attract goodwill, self-confidence, discernment, inspiration; (elixir by type); *Black:* redirect restlessness into productivity; *Blue:* clear speech, unblock mind/emotion, rubbing generates an electrical charge to direct energy; *Green/Black:* prosperity, deflect negative energies; *Green:* setting reasonable goals; Pink: encourage creativity, free the personality; *Watermelon:* encourage practical approach to manifesting ideas; *Watermelon/Pink:* self-understanding

Turquoise: verbal communication, put thoughts into words, protect the spirit, health, love, joy, social life, meditation, intuition, unify spiritual and physical; (open awareness, find creative solutions to problems, curb fear of the dark)

Zircon: spiritual sight, spiritual understanding

6

Spells and Divinations

Using the Tools

The various tools of Witchcraft were described in chapter 2, but in the actual practice of magic, the tools require the combination of energy and intent from the Witch to work properly. In order for a desired goal to be achieved, a Witch must be able to draw up the energy and direct it, and this is where the tool comes in as a focusing device. The athame and the wand act as a conduit of your energy flow, and, except for ritual functions, may be interchanged. You can cast a Circle with either one, but you can only use the knife, not the wand, in the chalice during the Cakes and Wine Ritual. The wand is the traditional tool most associated with Witches and Witchcraft, and it can be a powerful instrument. When the energy is raised, it passes through you and into the wand, and when you touch the tip of the wand to a spell item, that item is charged with the energy, while waving the wand will spread the energy through the air.

Getting familiar with the wand and athame means learning to feel energy. A simple exercise for this begins with sitting comfortably on the ground or floor, with your hands in your lap or on your knees. Ground and center, drawing up Earth energy through your body and visualizing the energy as a white swirl passing through each energy center: base of the spine, abdomen, navel, heart, throat, third eye, and top of the head. Let that energy flow back down and cycle up again so you are balanced and filled with energy. Rub your hands together, then move them apart a little distance and slowly bring them back close without touching. You should be able to feel some degree of resistance, and this is energy. Now move your hands to be parallel to the floor, and slowly push downward. Again, you will be able to feel some resistance. Refocus to visualize drawing energy upward from the Earth into your palms, seeing rays of energy being sucked upward if that helps, then slowly push the energy back down again.

Draw up energy into your hands again and slowly move your hands to form an energy ball, about the size of a cantaloupe. Focus into the center of that ball a simply stated desire that you can then release into the universe by tossing the energy ball into the air, releasing it with your open hands.

Now hold the wand in both hands, draw up Earth energy through your body again, and focus on it passing into the wand. Now slowly raise the wand and feel the energy move upward, then slowly lower the wand and feel the energy follow the path of the wand. Point the wand downward and release the energy back into the Earth through the tip of the wand. Set it down and do the same with the athame, then set it down, ground and center to bring your internal energies into balance, and release the excess energy. Handle your wand and athame often to imprint them with your psychic energy patterns. When casting the Circle, take the time to see the energy as a blue light shooting out of the end of the athame or wand to spread into an encompassing sphere around you while you are defining the diameter of the sacred space. There is no need to rush through a magical event.

If you have trouble with visualization, try grounding and centering when sitting comfortably, then going through a familiar process in your mind, seeing every step you normally take. As an example, if you ride a bicycle around the neighborhood, go through all the motions in your mind, paying attention to every detail—think about the pedals, the wheels, the handlebars, the seat, the chain, the bumps on the road, the sounds, scents, and sights along the way, your own breathing, the sensation in your muscles, the glare of the Sun or patches of shade from tree shadows, and so forth. It may take several journeys before you have everything right, and then you can start to take notice of the places you pass as you pedal. Another technique is to visualize every detail of peeling and eating an orange or an apple, incorporating the senses of sight, sound, texture, smell, and taste as you go through the process. Visualization will help you see the energy you are moving for magic, and it will help you to focus on how that energy will work to your benefit. Many spell materials function through pictures, so when you are able to project the picture of what you want to accomplish into the spell items, the energies are able to respond.

The other tools of your Craft will become imbued with your personal energy signature through use, so store or cover these when not working with them to avoid absorption of random energies. When you buy tools at a store, especially crystals and stones, the tools will have some degree of chaotic energy from all the activity in the store and being handled by people from the gathering process through packing, and shipping, to being placed on display and touched by store customers. Setting the object in sea salt or rock salt for three days soothes the object and cleanses it of extraneous energies so you can then make the tool ready for your use with the consecration in chapter 3.

Spell Construction

The way you put together your spells is determined by what you want to accomplish, and includes what you will say, the steps you will follow, the timing, and an approach that is consistent with the goal and the method. Spells are the vehicles of magical workings, so any ritual, brew, charm, chant, prayer, amulet, talisman, or crafted item created for magical purpose, utilizing the movement of energy, and the speaking of a word or formula (phrase), in the generating of intent into manifestation is a spell. You can inscribe a candle near the top so that as the symbol is melted, the magic is released, or use a pin to designate on the candle that when it melts that far the spell is sent into action, then chant, shake a rattle, dance, or meditate on the goal while the candle burns down to the pin. You can write down a goal and burn the paper in the candle flame during the spell casting, seeing the spell as sent on its way as it is consumed by the flame. You can burn herbs in the candle flame, stating the name of the herb and the purpose for which you are using it, seeing the energy released to perform the task assigned.

You can combine items into pouches to place somewhere or carry with you, stating the function of each thing used, and focusing on the desired outcome as you place the items into the pouch, or as you sew or tie it up. Because there are so many options available, you need to trust your intuition as you think about the desired outcome and see what method comes to mind, perhaps as you flip through the lists of correspondences in your Book of Shadows.

When you decide on the method of spell casting, stay focused as you raise and send energy to accomplish your goal. You do not need drugs or alcohol to create an altered state of awareness, but will have better results using meditation, breathing, chanting, dancing, and other such exercises. Raise energy only when the spell item is completely prepared and ready for empowerment and activation. Gathered energy needs to be released in one quick jolt once a peak is reached, so do not delay this as the energy will begin to dissipate. Learning the peak time for energy release is something that comes with practice. You will definitely feel it when the energy dwindles or wanders.

The moving of energy for magic requires that it be raised, focused on the intent of the spell, directed into the spell materials with a motion of your hands, wand, or athame, and sent on its way to accomplish the task with a sweeping motion of your hands, wand, or athame.

Your hands are tools for beseeching, invoking, blessing, signifying union with the energies, drawing energy inward, and extending inner energies outward to share. The palms absorb and release energy, so the hands are used, with or without a wand or athame, to gather the energies you are calling upon and to direct these energies into the spell materials. With both hands, you can focus the raised energy into a palpable ball, push the energy into the spell object, and send it off in the general direction needed for the spell to work or upward into the Universe for action. By dancing around the Circle, with your arms raised and palms open, you gather in energy from both the Earth and the Universe to supplement your own in spell casting.

As part of your spell work, you may address the Elementals at the quarters, either with the spell material in your hands, or by motioning the Elemental to the spell items from the four directions, with Earth giving strength to the spell for manifestation, Air moving it swiftly, Fire adding power to it, and Water bringing it to a satisfying conclusion. The Elementals may also be envisioned as the Four Winds, and so the North Wind may be addressed for physical actions, the East Wind for mental actions, the South Wind for vigorous actions, and the West Wind for emotional actions.

By ending your spell with "So Mote It Be!" or "It is Done!" you are affirming the goal as accomplished. You may want to say, "As I

Will," before the affirmation, just to emphasize that this is what you want. Once you have sent the energy off to perform its task, this statement also offers a sense of closure, so you will not hold back any of the raised energy. You should see it as gone, not hovering about. Then you touch the ground or floor with your palms to get your energy flow back into balance, letting go of extraneous energies. Remember that energy is cyclic, and once it has finished its task in a spell, the energy will return to the Earth for redistribution as Nature sees fit.

Candle Magics

Candle spells are very popular because they are so versatile. The color and the essential oil with which it is rubbed, the herbs added, the stones or crystals placed in or around it, the sigils and runes etched into the wax are all easy and effective methods of working a candle. All of these elements must be coordinated through the lists of correspondences so you do not create a conflict of energies. The color matches the intent, as does the oil, the runic symbols, herbs, or stones. You are focused on the desired outcome while you work the candle, using visualization to bring the result into manifestation. Be sure you know what it is you want, so that as your spell is conducted, you are using the raised energy in a manner consistent with the candle and other spell materials. If you like, you can write out the intent and then toward the end of the spell, burn it in the candle flame to release it into being.

While working the candle, you envision the power going into it, seeing the effect occurring then and there, so that when the spell ends, the effect is seen as done. To use herbs or stones in the candle, drop each one in separately, stating what power you want drawn from the item to work with the candle spell. A simple statement works easiest: "Mint for money." Do not drop a lot of herbal leaves into a candle lest you put it out—a pinch is sufficient. As you add things to the flame, the candle will melt faster, you will see the energies building in power, and when it feels to you that the power is strongest, you release the energies by directing them to your goal. Waving the wand in a circle above the candle gathers the energies in tightly, or you may let the candle burn while you dance (twirl deosil to gain or widdershins to disperse) around the Circle, and continue until the energy level is at the highest you can tolerate. This is when you stop in front of the burning candle, and with the wand (or power hand if not carrying the wand) throw the raised energy in to the candle and direct it with a key word or short phrase. With candle spells, you are normally sending the power out to have an effect in another location or in the Universe for the spell to be complete. See the spell as done, the effect achieved, then let the candle burn for an hour. Snuff it out (cover with a candle snuffer or a lid for the cauldron in which the candle is sitting), then look at the forms in the wax, and compare what you see to the purpose of the spell and the list of symbols (further in this chapter).

Once the candle cools, you can remove the waxy remains as described in chapter 3, then bury the remains in the ground, toss into moving water, or dispose of it in the garbage with the visualization that it will enter the ground through a landfill. If using the garbage, be sure to remove it from your living area, perhaps placing the garbage bag in the garage or on a porch until time for the pickup.

If dedicating a tall candle or using a seven-day knobby candle for a purpose, then you would simply rub it with an oil and light it, let a portion burn, snuff it, and then burn it some more over a period of several days. The seven-day candles are good for this and should be burned at the proper hour each day for the purpose. Dispose of any remains as usual. While you can reuse a candle in which no herbs have been used, this would require you to designate on the candle that once it burns past a mark, the spell is released. Then you can terminate the function of the candle when it cools by passing it through the Elemental symbols (salt, incense smoke, white or red candle flame, and water), cleanse it with running water, and store it for reuse.

Some Sample Spells

Meditation Spell

Perform during: Waxing to Full Moon; day of Sun, Moon, or Mercury; hour of Mercury or Sun.

Materials: light blue candle; sandalwood incense; seating pillow or chair.

Spell casting: Light incense and candle prior to beginning meditation; ground and center. Move your power hand in a direct line from the top of the head to the center of the tummy, turning your hand as you proceed so as to set it lightly upon the other hand as it rests palm up in the lap. For two counts each, breathe in, hold a moment, release through the mouth, and hold a moment. Repeat two more times, cleansing the lungs. Envision a shimmering white light radiating from the crown of the head:

> *I call upon the Powers of the Universe to aid me in*
> *my meditation.*

Begin the intended meditation. If there is a lot of remaining candle, as with a pillar style, let it cool, then wrap the candle in a blue cloth and store so you can light it again at your next meditation session. Otherwise, bury the candle remains or toss out with trash, with the visualization that it will be buried in landfill.

Blessed Water Recipe

Perform during: Full Moon Esbat; hour of Moon, Mercury, Mars, or Sun.

Materials: water in a cup or pitcher, empty bowl, rose (petals, water, or extract), salt, small mirror (compact style), a jar with a lid. You can make a sufficient amount to store for use in spell workings between Esbats.

Spell casting: Raise arms under Moonlight:

> *I call upon you, Great Lady, to bless this water I*
> *pour beneath your Lunar Light.*

Pour the water into the bowl, add a little rose petal and hold bowl up so the Moon light shines on the surface of the water:

> *In this water shines your Moon Light, reflecting your*
> *own light that this water be made consecrate in your*
> *sight. This water is cleansed and purified through*
> *your light on this Full Moon night.*

Lift the salt in the Moonlight:

> *Through the Lady do all things take their form;*
> *from the salt in the waters and the salt in the lands*
> *of the Earth. Through the bright Moon light, I do*
> *consecrate this salt to aid in my work.*

Add three pinches of salt to the water; stir three times; then use the mirror to reflect the Full Moon onto the water in the bowl:

> *By the light of the Moon, through the power in your*
> *Tides, a portion of your power now herein resides,*
> *that blessed be this water. By three times three this*
> *spell I bind, that it be cast with the power of nine.*
> *That as I will, So Mote It Be!*

Set down the mirror and the bowl and turn the bowl nine times deosil with the Moon reflected on the surface of the water:

> *With power gathered and sent within, this spell is*
> *sealed nine times again, that adds together nine*

*once more, that with these three is nine the core. So
Mote It Be!*

Pour the water into the jar and tighten the lid. Store away from
light, and use as blessed (or holy) water whenever needed.

Sacred Space Purification Spell

Perform during: Waxing to Full Moon; day of Moon or Sun; hour
of Moon, Saturn, or Mars.

Materials: small cook pot or aromatherapy bowl, blessed water,
1 star anise, 1 bay leaf, 1 teaspoon sage, burner or tealight heat
source; frankincense incense.

Spell casting: Consecrate an aromatherapy bowl or small cooking pot by passing it through the smoke of frankincense and
sprinkling with blessed water:

*I consecrate this container to aid in my Craft, that
the spell I now weave will take hold and last.*

Heat spring water in the bowl over a tealight or in the pot on a
burner. When the water is hot, add star anise:

*By the power of the star, let all negativity be
deflected from this place.*

Add bay leaf:

*As the scent of this leaf moves through this place,
may purification enter into this space.*

Add sage:

*Through sage I now make this spell manifest, that
with peace and protection this space will be blessed.
That as I will, So Mote It Be!*

Let the scent move through area for one hour, then dispose of
contents and wash out container.

New House Purification Spell

Perform during: Waning Moon; hour of Mars (prior to occupancy is best).

Materials: 2 red candles, mortar and pestle, herbs: bay leaf, yarrow flowers, basil leaves, rosemary leaves, St. Johnswort leaves, juniper berries, mullein leaves; charcoal disk; cauldron with a handle; peeled garlic cloves (1 for each room); plastic baggy with a twist tie.

Spell casting: Open all the windows in the house. Set red candles on either side of cauldron on kitchen counter and light. Light a charcoal disk and place inside the cauldron. Grind (with mortar and pestle) or crumble equal parts of bay leaf, basil leaves, yarrow flowers, rosemary leaves, St. Johnswort leaves, juniper berries, and the mullein. Add the herbs to the glowing charcoal:

> *I call upon you magical herbs to drive out negativity and chaos, bringing your blessings of peace and concord to this place.*

Peel the garlic cloves and place one in the center of each room:

> *I call upon you good garlic to gather into yourselves the negativity and chaos that lingers, to draw into yourselves all malefic vapors and energies.*

Carry the cauldron from room to room, censing each room widdershins, then return the cauldron to the countertop between the candles. Vacate the house for thirteen minutes, then return and gather the garlic cloves into a plastic bag without touching them (turn the bag inside-out and use as a glove for your hand as you pick up the cloves, then holding them in your fist, pull the bag back over your hand and release the cloves so they are inside the bag and your hand is not), fasten with the twist tie, and put it outside in the trash. Close the windows and let the candles burn another hour, then snuff them. Scatter the cooled incense remains out of doors; bury candle remains or toss out in the trash (envisioning them as being buried in a landfill) and keep these remains out of the house until garbage day.

Home Protection Spell

Perform during: Waxing to Full Moon; day of Moon, Mars or Saturn; hour of Mars or Saturn.

Materials: a few stems of any combination of the following herbs: dill, fennel, mint, marjoram, mustard, mullein, mustard, rosemary, rue, white heather, woodruff, and yarrow; red thread.

Spell casting: Tie small bundles of herbs together with red thread and place on the altar. Touch with the tip of the athame:

> *I conjure thee, protective herbs, on this day of*
> *(planet) and at this hour of (planet), to be a protec-*
> *tion and safeguard against all adversity and evil.*
> *Protect well this house and all who dwell within.*
> *That as I will, So Mote It Be!*

Hang one bundle in each room of the home. Replace the bundles each year, scattering the used herbs in the wind or putting the bundles in the trash.

Protection Pouch

Perform during: Waning to New Moon; day of Saturn; hour of Mars, Saturn, or Sun.

Materials: black cloth; needle and red thread; tsp. of agrimony, clove, blackthorn; cauldron; wand; athame; pentacle; you may add an appropriate stone such as jasper to the pouch with a statement of its purpose, such as "protection."

Spell casting: Sew a small pouch with the black cloth and red thread. Place the herbs into the cauldron:

*Agrimony to return negative energies to the sender.
Blackthorn to deflect negative energies away from
me. Clove to exorcise harmful energies from my
presence.*

Stir with the tip of athame:

*Three herbs I call to work for me; harnessing nega-
tive energy; take and bind and send away; harmful
forces in my way.*

Stuff the herbs into the little pouch, (add stone if desired:
"With jasper to keep me well protected.") then sew it up and set it
on the pentacle. Wave the wand over pouch, then touch to pouch:

*Earth and Air, Fire and Water! Emanations of the
Lady and the Lord! I call upon thy grace and love to
seal protection in this ward!*

Carry the pouch in a pocket, purse, briefcase, etc. as desired, or
place inside the glove compartment or under the driver's seat in
your car.

Money Spell

Perform during: Waxing to Full Moon of each Quarter [December,
March, June, September]; day of Jupiter; hour of Saturn.

Materials: a dollar bill, silver and gold candles for the Goddess
and God; green working candle; patchouli oil; cauldron to hold
melted wax of votive and to burn the dollar bill in, lid or covering
to snuff flame.

Spell casting: Light the silver and gold candles. Rub patchouli
oil on the green candle and inscribe with: ♭, ⸕, $, ♄, ♃, ☽, ☉.
Set the green candle in the cauldron and light. Burn the dollar bill
in the candle flame, while rotating the cauldron nine times:

With Saturn, Jupiter, and the Sun;
As Lunar cycles spin endlessly;
God of gold, laughing and free;
Lady of silver, dancing with me;
Bring me thy power, fill up my bower;
Bring me this Season, abundant money!

Bury the candle remains or toss out in trash, and repeat the spell each season.

Money Candle Spell

Perform during: Waxing to Full Moon; day of Mercury, Jupiter, or Sun; hour of Mercury or Jupiter.

Materials: patchouli incense, 1 green votive candle, a cauldron to hold green candle and melted wax, 3 deity candles (blue, white, and orange), wand, athame, pentacle, bergamot oil, a bowl to mix herbs, herbs (a pinch of each): allspice, bergamot, comfrey, chamomile, cinquefoil, whole cloves, nutmeg, mint, marjoram (you may use a simmering potpourri of water instead of candle and cauldron if desired). Light the deity candles and incense.

Spell casting: Empower the herbs by mixing in a bowl with the athame, then passing the bowl through the symbols of the Elementals:

I call upon you Elemental Powers to charge these
herbs and bring forth their energies to work with me
in the spell I cast! Herbs be now charged by Elemen-
tal Earth [sprinkle with salt]; *by Elemental Air* [pass
through incense smoke]; *by Elemental Fire* [pass
through the flame of the center white candle]; *and*
by Elemental Water [sprinkle with blessed water or
with spring water].

Set the cauldron or potpourri on the pentacle. Rub the green candle with bergamot oil and inscribe the wax with these symbols: ᛒ, ᚠ, ᛏ, ᚠ, ᚠ, ᛉ, and ᛉ. Set the candle in the cauldron, light it, and then slowly, a little at a time, drop the herbs into the flame (or into the simmering potpourri water):

> *With the power of Air is the spell carried; with the power of Fire is the magic released.*

Sprinkle a little of the water, being careful not to extinguish the candle:

> *With the power of Water is the will spread.*

Add a tiny tipful of salt with the athame:

> *And with the power of Earth is the goal brought into being.*

Move wand widdershins three times over the green candle or pot pourri:

> *As this spell spreads through the air; nothing may my work impair! Bring success and wealth to me; That As I Will, So Mote It Be!*

Let the candle or potpourri burn for one hour, then snuff and scry for signs in the melted wax or the placement of the herbal remains (see "Tea Leaf Reading" in this chapter for symbols of divination). Bury the candle wax or toss it out in trash, or wash out the potpourri container.

Car Protection Spell

Perform during: Waxing to Full Moon; day of Jupiter, Saturn, or Sun; hour of Jupiter, Saturn, or Sun.

Materials: a square of light blue cotton cloth, a tablespoon of betony, 3 mustard seeds, 1 teaspoon of fennel seed, a tablespoon of St. Johnswort, red string, 3 white feathers, 9 silver and black beads, incense of dragon's blood, frankincense, or patchouli, a red candle, a cauldron, blessed water, and salt.

Spell casting: Light the incense. Inscribe the red candle with: ᚦ , ᚾ, ᛉ, ᛁ, ᚤ, ᛒ, ᛗ, ᚣ , ᛩ , set it in the cauldron and light. On the cloth square place the betony and mustard seeds:

> *Betony and Mustard Seed for their protective*
> *energies!*

Add the fennel seeds and St. Johnswort:

> *Fennel and St. Johnswort for their power and*
> *strength!*

Tie the ends of the cloth together with the red string:

> *Red for might!*

Pass the pouch through the symbols of the Elementals:

> *I call upon thee Elementals to charge this spell and*
> *bring forth the Power to work with me as I have*
> *cast! Be you charged pouch of protection, by Ele-*
> *mental Earth* [sprinkle with salt], *by Elemental Air*
> [pass through the incense smoke]*; by Elemental*
> *Fire* [pass through the red candle flame]*; and by Ele-*
> *mental Water* [sprinkle with blessed or spring water].

Decorate the pouch with the feathers:

> *I call upon you, mighty Wind, for your blessing*
> *upon this charm!*

Decorate the pouch with the beads:

> *I call upon you, mighty Earth, for your blessings*
> *upon this charm!*

Open the Circle and take the pouch to the car. Walk around the car, touching the pouch to the front, back, and sides of the car:

*Let the protective powers within this pouch bring
safe travel, power, and strength to this vehicle!*

Place the pouch in the glove compartment, or under the front
seat, or hang it from the rearview mirror for protection of the car.
Snuff the red candle and bury the remains in the ground or wrap
and place in the trash to be buried in a landfill.

Health Spell

Perform during: Waxing to Full Moon; day of Mars, Jupiter, or
Sun; hour of Jupiter.

Materials: sandalwood incense, Goddess and God candles; 2
yellow votive candles; 2 containers for votives that will hold
melted wax; rue oil; salt; blessed water; a pinch each of ash bark,
St. Johnswort, tansy, woodruff, and an herb that most relates to
the specific illness from your herbal list of correspondences.

Spell crafting: Anoint the yellow votives with rue oil:

> *These candles are dedicated to the healing of* _____,
> *in the Names of the Lady and the Lord* _____ *and*
>
> _____.

Pass the yellow votives through the symbols of the Elementals:

> *I consecrate these through the power of Elemental
> Earth* [sprinkle with salt], *through the power of Ele-
> mental Air* [pass through incense smoke], *through
> the power of Elemental Fire* [pass through the flames
> of both Deity candles], *and through the power of El-
> emental Water* [sprinkle with blessed water].

Inscribe both yellow candles with ᛒ, ᚠ, ᚺ, ᚦ , ᛏ, ᛟ, ᚡ, ᚾ, ᚲ,
ᚦ, and ᛉ .

Light one candle from the Goddess candle and one from the
God candle.

Add the following herbs into the flames of each votive candle:

> *Ash bark for health and protection; St. Johnswort*
> *for health, protection, and strength; tansy for health*
> *and the love of the Goddess; woodruff for victory*
> *and the love of the God; (ailment-related herb) or*
> *the healing of (name or type of ailment).*

Let the votive candles burn until reduced nearly to the bottom of the container. Snuff out, then scry the wax. Bury the remains or toss out in trash seeing it as being buried in a landfill.

Regain Good Health Spell

Perform during: Waxing to Full Moon; day of Mars, Jupiter, or Sun; hour of Jupiter.

Materials: peppermint oil, 1 light blue votive candle, cauldron, herbs: 2 tsp. lavender flower and 1 tsp. each of thyme, allspice, coriander seed, and willow leaf

Spell casting: Grind the herbs together:

> *I charge you by the Sun and the Moon, on this day*
> *of high energy and hour of healing, to release your*
> *powers into my work!.*

Rub peppermint oil on the light blue votive candle. Inscribe the candle with the symbols of Earth, Air, and Fire: ▽ △ △, then add a word for the ailment. Draw the following symbols in the candle while doing the incantation:

> *Jupiter (♃) for health, Beorc (ᛒ) for the Goddess,*
> *Water (▽) for fluids, Tyr (↑) for victory, Osa (ᚠ)*
> *for the God, and Sigel (ᛋ) to direct the healing*
> *energy.*

Set the candle in the cauldron and light:

*I call upon thee Great Goddess to hasten my healing.
Through this candle dedicated to Health, inscribed
with the symbols of the God and the Goddess; Healing Energy and Victory over the Watery confusion
in my body, and with the herbs of healing whose
energy may be released to my aid do I call upon You.
Cast aside my sickly imbalance, I bid you, That As I
Will, So Mote It Be!*

Add the herbal mixture:

*With the protective cleansing power of lavender;
with the healing strength of thyme, allspice, and
coriander seed, and with the protective and healing
power of the willow do I infuse this spell with the
power to work my will. So Mote It Be!*

Burn the votive for one hour, then snuff and scry the wax for
images indicating the response time, then bury the remains or
toss out in trash to be buried in a landfill.

Divinations

Divinations are a familiar part of Witchcraft, being both a means
of communicating with the Divine and the Elementals of Nature,
and a type of meditation for self-improvement. The events and
influences shown in any divination indicate how things are lined
up at the time of the reading, so that if you do not like what you
see, you can make changes to affect the outcome. Divination also
affords the reader with the advantage of having an idea of how a
situation in question currently stands—sometimes even hidden
matters surface and offer a warning or support for intended actions. When applied to daily life, the readings are short and basic,
intended only to provide a general feel for the type of energy affecting the day. Once you know something even this simple, you

are prepared for how things may flow, and understand what to encourage or what to avoid or to discourage. There are many types of divination, and some people prefer one to another, but it is good to try a few of these out and learn more than one. Should you be asked for a divination by another person, be certain first that you have a good understanding of what you are doing and that the person is not fearful. Be sure to let the person know that the energies evident may be changed, or situations averted—no one wants to hear doom and gloom with no reprieve. The reality is that the signs and symbols are subject to change, and sometimes just being aware is sufficient to alter matters.

Numerology

Numerology has a variety of uses aside from divination, but it factors into this, as well as how you conduct spell work and understand the interconnections between people, times, and events. You can choose the timing for your spells according to the numerical influence of the date, month, year, or hour and use this as your focus based upon the needs of the spell, which is handy should you be unable to fit a spell in an hour with the desired planetary influence. So instead of seeing in your mind that the hour relates to a planetary energy, you visualize the energy of the number of the hour from your list of numerical associations. The way to determine how to find the optimal number for your magical work is through reducing the relevant numbers to a base number of 1 through 9, using a double-digit base number, or using 12 or 13. The number may be derived in a very straightforward manner, such as needing a spell for health and deciding to work the magic at 3:00 P.M. since the number 3 relates to Jupiter and to health. Although the day of the week may be Wednesday, the day of Mercury, and that hour is influenced by Venus on the planetary chart (if sunrise is at 7 A.M., for example), your mind is not focused on these energies, but on the energy of the number 3. Suppose you want to do a spell to aid in making a decision, but neither the day of the week or the hour relates to this type of energy. If the date is the 15th, you could focus on the numerical energy of 1+5=6, and this affords the correct centering energy. You can use the numbers instead of the planetary hours or days, but there has to be an idea of reasonable association for this to work.

Numbers are also distilled from names by adding together the numbers that correlate to letters of the alphabet. The digits of the sum are then added again until reduced to a single digit number. The name Joan can be written with the numerical values of $1 + 6 + 1 + 5 = 13$, which is reduced by adding $1 + 3 = 4$. Thus the name "Joan" has a numerical value of 4. Middle names and last names are treated the same way, and the numbers of all three names are added and reduced to find the number that most relates to a person. A person can apply their name number to match the numbers in their life, from home address to occupation, to wedding date and other important events.

The birthdate is an important number, and when reduced to a single digit number, indicates a person's life pattern. The number is derived by adding the month as numbered 1 through 12, the day of birth, and the year of birth. By relating the final reduced number to a Major Arcana tarot card (covered later in this chapter), you see the energy influencing your life. If you were born on January 12, 1980, your number is derived from $1 + 1 + 2 = 4$, 1980 $+ 4 = 1984$, $1 + 9 + 8 + 4 = 22$, $2 + 2 = 4$. The interesting thing about relating the life number to the Major Arcana of the tarot is that there are 22 cards to work with, and so if your month, day, and year add up to a number 10 to 22, you have two influencing numbers, with the double-digit number offering an additional clue to your personality, and the single-digit number showing the life pattern. The number 22 in this example relates to the 0 in the tarot, since the Major Arcana numbers are 1 through 21, but there are 22 cards, thus the Fool card may be at the start or finish of the

Major Arcana. This card represents a personality that thrives with new beginnings, is courageous and bold, and possesses an eager enthusiasm. The number 4 relates to the Emperor, and shows that fulfillment in the life pattern would come from building something for which one is personally responsible. The two cards together would be excellent for someone who desires to run an independent business, as an example.

Two-digit numbers can be used for their mystical value, such as 13 as the number of the Goddess; 12 for working with the Fair Folk or having the grounding and foundational energy of 3 times 4; and 10 for success and completion. Double digit numbers such as 11, 22, 33, 44, etc. offer a double emphasis of the main number. Double numbers may be recited in a spell as 2 by 2 or 3 by 3, etc., for a balance afforded by the energy of two combined with the energy of the digits. Triple numbers are used for bindings; quadruple numbers are used for squaring and setting—making the value of the number a foundation (4) for a spell. These multiples are used mainly in knot magics, wherein each knot tied binds the energy of the spell. The following listing of the *base numbers* of 1 through 9 shows the letters (for determining the numerical association of names), the astrological and Elemental energy, and the basic areas of influence.

Number Correspondences

1 = letters A, J, S; Sun; Fire; developing the Self, the Universal All, initiation and conclusion, wholeness, and unity

2 = the letters B, K, T; Moon; Water; sensitivity and personality, truth, duality, blessing, and balance

3 = the letters C, L, U; Jupiter; Fire; health and opportunity, triads and triple aspects, and career

4 = the letters D, M, V; Uranus; Air; divination and knowledge, the Quarters, firmness, strength, foundations, and the Elementals

5 = the letters E, N, W; Mercury; Air; communication, the five-fold aspect of the pentagram as the Elementals and Spirit connection, and fulfillment

6 = the letters F, O, X; Venus; Earth; sociability and the Emotions, the Triple Goddess and the Triple God together, magnetism, cats, and decisions

7 = the letters G, P, Y; Neptune; Water; the subconscious, intuition, psychic power, mysticism, dual triads united, and change

8 = letters H, Q, Z; Saturn; Earth; freedom, dual foundations, material and spiritual worlds, law, self-discipline, travel and news

9 = the letters I, R; Mars; Fire; aggression, energy, new path, immortality, indestructibility, and a binding to completion

Tea Leaf Reading

To read tea leaves, you make a pot of tea with loose leaf tea, then pour into a cup without straining the leaves. You drink almost all of the tea, sometimes focusing on a particular question or desired information, or simply allowing your energies to seep into the tea through your handling of the teacup for a general reading. When you have only a little tea left in the cup, swirl it around the cup three times, then turn the cup upside-down on the saucer. With the handle of the cup closest to you, turn the cup three times deosil, return it to an upright position with the handle again closest to you—at the 6:00 position.

Now you look at the pattern of the leaves along the inside and bottom of the cup, examining them for symbols or recognizable forms. The reading proceeds deosil from the handle, with the timing closest to the present at the left side of the handle. Things closest to the rim are read as locations that are further away, while those closest to the bottom are nearby. A variation of this technique is to have the *querant* (questioner) drink the tea, then hand the cup and saucer to the reader who swirls the tea, upends the cup, turns it, sets it upright again, and does the reading. Use the list of symbols for ideas as to what the patterns mean.

Symbolism For Divination

Symbols are found in the arrangement of tea leaves, melted wax and other residue of spell work, cloud formations, patterns of smoke, leaves, birds in flight or on the ground, swirling water, and so forth. Nearly anything can serve as a tool for divination; simply ask the question on your mind and look to see the answer. Sometimes there will be images that relate to a specific event, or as a sign to take notice of something, in which case, the image may be more an event picture than a symbol of something. Usually, the symbols found in divinations such as tea leaf reading and other types of scrying represent a deeper meaning and so if, as an example, you see a rose in the pattern, this could mean you will get or see a rose that draws your attention, or more likely it could relate to love or healing.

The list that follows provides meanings for some typical symbols, but it is intended only as a guideline. Since all perception is filtered through individual senses, memories, and associations, the symbols may have different nuances for you than for other people. There are also other images that you might see that are not listed, in which case, you need to trust your intuition. For example, a clump of tea leaves in a cup may remind you of a badger, and since it is not on the list, you have to consider what a badger means to you. One person may think of an attacking foe, since the animal is easily provoked to bite and attack, while another might think of security and protection since the animal is fiercely protective of its burrow. A symbol must be read through the intuitive facility of the reader, and in conjunction with the other symbols seen with it, as with tea leaf reading, or in relation to the purpose or question of the divination, as with melted wax forms after spell work or interpretation of clouds, smoke, etc. after asking a question. If the meanings offered here do not work for you, then feel free to adjust them in accordance with your own personal approach. Having trust in your own intuition is part of Witchcraft, for it is through this subconscious medium that the communication of divination takes place.

Acorn—youth, strength, man, small start for large accomplishment

Airplane—travel, new projects

Anchor—voyage, rest, problem solved

Arrow—news, disagreements, direct action

Basket—gift, security, comfort

Baby—new interests, security, new beginnings

Bees (hive, comb)—fertility, industry, community, self-sacrifice

Bell—celebrations, news (good or bad, depending on other indicators)

Bird—psychic power, flight, luck, friendship end, communication

Boat—discoveries, travel, companionship

Book—wisdom, learning

Bottle—celebration, success

Broom—Goddess, purification, healing, end of a problem, changes

Bridge—crossing to new endeavors, transition, partnership, travel

Butterfly—the soul, spiritual contact, frivolity, insincerity

Castle—financial gain, security, inheritance, life of bounty

Cage—isolation, restriction, imprisonment, containment

Camel—long journey, need to conserve energy or goods, relocation

Cat—wisdom, spiritual access, female friend, domestic strife

Car—local travel, movement in business affairs, overcome obstacles

Cauldron—Goddess, transformation, endings/new beginnings, vitality

Candle—illumination, innovation, inspiration

Clock—time indicated for a spell's completion, change

Chair—relaxation, pause, comfort, entertainment

Clouds—mental activity, thoughtfulness, problems, hidden obstacles

Coffin—end of a matter, lengthy but not serious illness

Clover—good fortune, success, rural location

Cow—money, property, comfort, tranquillity

Cradle—newcomers, beginning of a new idea or project

Crescent—Goddess, wish granted, newness, freshness

Cornucopia—Goddess, abundance, fertility, prosperity, protection

Cross—(Solar) God, nature works with power; (Roman) suffering, conflict

Cup—love, harmony, close friendship, gift

Dagger—complications, dangers, power, skill

Death/dying—birth, marriage, long life, prosperity

Distaff—creativity, changes, sexuality

Dog—fidelity, friendship, companionship, faithfulness

Duck—plenty, wealth, success

Elephant—advice needed, obstacles overcome, good luck

Egg—increase, fertility, luck, creativity, new start, hoarding

Eye—introspection, awareness, evaluation, spirit

Fan—indiscretion, disloyalty, things hidden, inflammations

Fish—riches, luck, sexuality, productivity

Flag—warning, defensiveness, identification with group/ideals

Flame, fire—purification, change, domination of the will

Flower—marriage, unhappy love affair, passing joy

Glove—protection, luck, aloofness, nobility, challenge

Gate—opportunity, advancement, change, new directions

Gun (any type)—power to gain goals, discord, slander, infidelity

Hammer—hard work rewarded, building, creativity, fortitude

Hat—honors, rivalry, independence, self-assertion

Hound—advice, help given, companionship, trust

Heart—love, pleasure, confidence, strength of will

Harp—contentment, spirituality

Horns—God, fertility, spirituality, forces of nature

Horse—travel, strength, work, grace, power, success, prosperity

Horseshoe—protection, luck, start of a new enterprise

Hourglass—caution, passage of time

House—security, authority, success, comfort

Key—understanding, mysteries, opportunity, gain, security

Kite—warning for caution, new ideas, plans made public

Knot—restrictions, marriage, bindings

Knife—duplicity, misunderstanding, direct action

Ladder—initiation, rise or fall in status, connections

Lion—power, strength, influence, ferocity, pride, domination

Lock—protection, concealment, security, obstacles, sealed

Man—visitor, helpful stranger

Mirror—reversal, knowledge, Karma

Moon—the Goddess, intuitive wisdom, guidance

Mountain—hindrance, challenge, obstacle, journey, steadfastness

Mouse—thriftiness, poverty, theft, frugality, inconspicuousness

Mushroom—shelter, food, business complications, Fairy contact

Nail—labor, construction, pain, unity

Owl—wisdom, spiritual communication

Palm tree—respite, relief, security, protection, blessings

Parrot—gossip, ostentatiousness

Peacock—luxury, vanity, arrogance—all with little foundation

Pineapple—hospitality, good things hidden by harsh exterior

Pipe—truth obscured, concentration, comfort, ease

Purse—monetary gain, possessions kept close

Ring—eternity, containment, wheel of life/year, wedding

Rose—love, lost or past love, fullness of life, healing, caring

Salt—purity, stability, cleansing, grounding

Scales—balance, justice, careful evaluation

Scissors—duplicity, arguments, separation, division, strife

Shell—Goddess, emotional stability, luck, artistic ability

Ship—travel, news, material gains, romance

Skull—consolation, comfort, personal hurts, endings and a new life

Snake—God and Goddess, wisdom, immortality, knowledge, prophecy

Spider—good luck, industry, entrapments, secrecy, cunning

Spoon—luck, sustenance, the basic needs of life secured

Sun—the God, success, energy, power

Star—good luck, divine protection, opportunity, success, destiny

Swan—good luck, love, evolving beauty, noble spirit

Sword—power, strife, conflict, overcoming adversity

Tree—blessings of Nature, good fortune, stability, power, security

Turtle—fertility, security, defense against obstacles, slow gains

Umbrella—temporary shelter, limited protection

Unicorn—purity, nature, Fairy blessings, Otherworld intervention

Well—blessing from the Goddess, inspiration, spirituality, health

Wheel—completion, eternity, season/life cycles, rebirth, gains

Windmill—business dealings, factors working together for one goal

The Tarot

Reading tarot cards has been associated with Gypsies and Witches for quite some time, and today there are numerous decks to choose from. The cards form a focus for divinations and consultations with the Divine, so while intuition may play a vital role in the readings, it is also important to know the generally accepted meanings for the cards. Cards are shuffled and cut, then laid out in a spread which may follow traditional patterns or be one of your own creation. The subject of tarot can fill a book by itself, as can most of the topics in this overview of Witchcraft, but you can still delve into the cards with a basic understanding. The tarot were originally only read upright, then in the nineteenth century the innovation of reverses was introduced. Since there are sufficient cards to show both positive and negative energy influences, only the upright is used here. If you want to use reverse meanings, then simply see the upright meanings as muted or delayed.

A tarot deck should be consecrated as with any tool, as already shown in chapter 3. Then the deck should be wrapped in cloth of a color you select according to the color correspondence chart (black, green, red are most commonly used). The material is traditionally silk, velvet, or cotton. Tarot bags with relevant designs are also available in stores and catalogs for storing the cards, as are tarot boxes. In the case of the latter, you should still wrap the cards before putting them in the box.

The tarot cards provide you with a tool of mediumship bringing you into contact with Universal Energy to address a particular question or problem, or to simply offer guidance and comfort. If you see a vision or sense a strong association for a card other than what is listed, follow your intuitive interpretation. The twenty-two cards of the Major Arcana (0–21) are the archetype cards showing cosmic and karmic destiny events and influences, while the Minor Arcana of fifty-six cards are the mundane cards relating to everyday events and influences. You can learn more about the individual cards by looking at one at a time, over a period of time, meditating on the card, and walking with the beings or images represented on each card. By walking with them in their setting and listening to what they may say or indicate through gesture and action, you are pathworking and adding to your understanding of what intuitive keys lie within the pictures. Select your tarot deck according to whether or not the images draw you, or speak to your intuitive mind.

Major Arcana Meanings

0—The Fool: Spontaneity, courageous, fresh start, excitement, carefree

1—The Magician: Communication, creativity, skill, astuteness, adaptability

2—The High Priestess: Secrets, intuition, esoteric wisdom, psychic abilities

3—The Empress: Bounty, fruitfulness, growth, inspiration, creativity, security

4—The Emperor: Builder, responsibility, stability, empowerment, productivity

5—The Hierophant: Organizing spirituality, inspiration, teacher, tradition, ritual

6—The Lovers: Choices, decision making, balance, partnership, trust

7—The Chariot: Victory, merit recognized, control, dominance, fast action, travel

8—Strength: Courage, fortitude, power, defeating obstacles

9—The Hermit: Wisdom, seeker, guide, personal growth, changing times

10—The Wheel of Fortune: Fortunes improve, success, opportunity, progress

11—Justice: Objective, balanced, fair, ethical, prevail in legal matter

12—The Hanged Man: Suspended activity, transition, meditation, vision questing

13—Death: Change, transformation, turning point, optimistic new start

14—Temperance: Harmony of mental/psychic states, blend of ideas, inspiration

15—The Devil: Freedom, choosing what appeals, following instincts

16—The Tower: Shocking event, sudden change/enlightenment, illusions go

17—The Star: Opportunity, wishes granted, hopes obtainable, inspiration

18—The Moon: Trust instincts, subconscious manifested, creativity, psychic

19—*The Sun:* Happiness, success, achievement, satisfaction

20—*Judgement:* Efforts rewarded, self-evaluation, transformation, renewal

21—*The World:* Completion, achievement, success, joy, conclusion and beginning

Suits for the Minor Arcana

The cards of the Minor Arcana are distributed between four suits, from which the modern playing cards of Ace through King evolved, with the Jack being a combination of Knight and Page from the tarot cards. The tarot has the suits of Pentacles, Swords, Wands, and Cups—these became the suits of Diamonds, Spades, Clubs, and Hearts of the familiar playing cards. Tarot decks use a variety of imagery for the suits, so here is a listing showing some common names, the Elemental connections, and what the suits represent:

Pentacles (Disks, Coins, Diamonds): *Elemental Earth* (North, winter, Midnight, green/brown, minerals, the material and physical)
Suit for: finances, money, business, material and physical matters and comfort

Swords (Knives, Spades): *Elemental Air* (East, spring, sunrise, yellow/white, Spirit, intellect, breath)
Suit for: strength, power, conflicts, worries, mental processes, and intellect

Wands (Rods, Staves, Clubs): *Elemental Fire* (South, summer, noon, orange/red, plant, insight, life-force)
Suit for: career, study, creative ventures, work, self, and Spirit

Cups (Bowls, Cauldrons, Hearts): *Elemental Water* (West, autumn, sunset, blue/indigo, animal, blood)
Suit for: emotions, intuition, psychic power, love, friendship, and feelings

Meanings for the Minor Arcana

Each card has special qualities, enhanced in modern tarot decks by the images depicted on the cards. By looking at the pictures, you can pull intuitive meanings from the cards, and by relating these images to the position they occupy in a spread (the pattern in which the cards are laid out on the table) or what cards they accompany, you can choose which interpretation fits the particular throw (shuffling, cutting the deck, and laying out the cards in a spread). Not all of the meanings for a given card apply in a particular reading, and you learn through practice how they interrelate. Some popular spreads use ten cards, which are laid out in various patterns, so here is a Celtic Cross spread with the meanings of the positions:

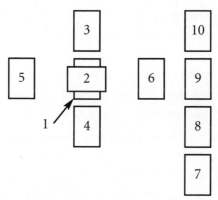

1 = where you are now
2 = current influences or obstacles
3 = goals
4 = foundation
5 = past
6 = future
7 = current environment or home
8 = strengths
9 = hopes/fears
10 = conclusion

The best way to use a spread like this is to focus on a question while shuffling the deck. If doing a reading for someone else, the person may simply knock on the deck prior to your shuffling the cards, or you may let the person handle the deck, shuffle the cards, or select ten cards after you shuffle, cut the deck by three, restack and fan out the cards on the table. When cutting the deck, hold the cards in one hand and set the deck on the table. Pick up all but a portion that feels right to you and set the deck next to the first stack. Pick up all but a portion again and set the remaining cards in a third stack. You now have three stacks next to each other. Pick up the middle stack, set it on top of the first stack, pick those up, and set on top of the last stack. Now you are ready to deal the cards out into a pattern and determine the meanings.

Another type of spread is to ask a "Yes or No" question, then after shuffling, cutting, and restacking the deck, begin counting out thirteen cards into three stacks, laying the cards face-up, but stopping one stack and moving to the next to start over with the count if an Ace comes between the first and thirteenth card. If you have thrown three stacks of thirteen cards each with no Aces, the answer is "No," but if you have three Aces, the answer is a definite "Yes," two Aces is "Yes," and look at the other card to see what influences this, and one Ace is a "Possibly," and look at the other two ending cards in the other two stacks to see what influences this. If the influences look very promising, such as the Sun and the Star, then you know the answer is actually a "Yes," and the interpretation shows that your dreams will be achieved.

The Elemental spread has five cards laid face-down:

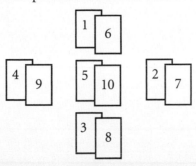

Then another five cards are laid over these, face-up, while focusing on a question. Card 6 shows the answer by Earth (manifestation), 7 shows the answer by Air (thoughts), 8 shows the answer by Fire (energy), 9 shows the answer by Water (emotions), and 10 shows the question in Spirit (intuitive Self). Cards 1–5 are then turned over to show the hidden influences behind the answers.

Pentacles

Ace: Commercial success, prosperity, material attainment, promotion

Two: New skills learned, balancing money, business decision, new job

Three: Celebrity, prestige, commitments, work rewarded, craftsmanship

Four: Financial security, private, budget, self-contained, withdrawn

Five: Financial worries, delayed income, unexpected expenses

Six: Gift or bonus, tempered generosity, financially self-confident

Seven: Gain by perseverance, nurturing a project, impatient for results

Eight: Commercial ability, enthusiasm with work, personal effort and skill

Nine: Accomplishment, self-esteem, good fortune, surprise gift

Ten: Prosperity, family heritage, stability, joy

Page: Turning an interest into a career, diligence in work, study

Knight: Propitious occasion, competence, reliable, hard worker

Queen: Plans realized, realistic ambitions, financial independence

King: Economic power, business/career success, ideas manifested, counselor

Swords

Ace: Victory, strength, power, determination, truth

Two: Tensions ease, balance of opposites, vital decision, diplomacy

Three: New unknown path, separation, unfinished business, conflicts

Four: Rest, vigilance, orderly peace, recuperation, cleansing, patience

Five: Injured self-esteem, forcefulness gains goals, honorable struggle

Six: Journey, leaving troubles behind, overcoming difficulties

Seven: Strategy, perseverance, tricky situation, clever approach

Eight: Dilemma, stay the course, patience needed, ignore rumor

Nine: Anxieties, unfounded worries, plans about to be realized

Ten: End of present troubles, proven ability to defend ideas, fresh start

Page: Insightful, readiness for action, communication skills, vigilance

Knight: Swift action, sudden changes, ability and courage, self-assured

Queen: Independent, insightful, perceptive, determined, language skills

King: Authority, legal action, implementing decisions, determination

Wands

Ace: Career start, creative awakening, new beginning, invention

Two: Boldness, fulfillment, earned success, seeking a new challenge.

Three: Good career news, negotiations, practical knowledge, teamwork

Four: Efforts rewarded, promotion, harmony, rejoicing, romance

Five: Competition and tests, struggle, teamwork needed

Six: Victory, public acclaim, triumph over obstacles

Seven: Advantage, defending a position, writer/student/teacher, courage

Eight: News from a distance, swift action, travel

Nine: Strength, readiness, security, project nears completion

Ten: Stress of success, over committed, need for delegation, tenacity

Page: Restlessness, resourceful, reliable, ambitious, important news

Knight: Looking for new adventure, enterprising activity, fearless explorer

Queen: Practical, optimistic, joyful, creative, imaginative, kindness

King: Professional cooperation, good counsel, conscientious, honesty

Cups

Ace: Abundance, joy, love, inspiration, emotional fulfillment

Two: Harmony, partnership, affection, marriage

Three: Celebration, good news, problems resolved, wedding, birth

Four: Reassessment, new possibilities, unidentified longings

Five: Useless regrets, disillusionment, partial loss, troubled legacy

Six: Nostalgia, manifesting past expectations, reunions

Seven: Choices, materialize dreams, truth revealed, evaluate plans

Eight: Turning point, new path, new direction in life, moderation

Nine: Wishes fulfilled, efforts rewarded, contentment, happy future

Ten: Contentment, recognition, esteem, good reputation, security

Page: Practical use of talents, creative inspiration, emotions satisfied

Knight: Opportunity, invitation, artistic ability, new insight, sensitive young man

Queen: Emotional truth, sensitive, psychic, nurturing, artistic

King: Responsible, reliable, counselor, creative, arts and sciences

Tarot Charts

You may want to create a handy chart on a note card to use while becoming familiar with the cards of the tarot. This will act as a prompt for you to recall the more detailed meanings and react to the scenes in the cards as well as the position of the card in the spread. Do not be afraid to create your own spreads, just be consistent and know what the placements mean for you. Experiment with the layouts and find what appeals to you. Here are sample key word charts for the Major and Minor Arcanas:

Major Arcana

0—The Fool	Spontaneity/Fresh Start
1—The Magician	Communication/Control of Destiny
2—The High Priestess	Secrets/Wisdom/Follow Intuition
3—The Empress	Abundance/Growth/Creativity
4—The Emperor	Builder/Responsibility/Productive
5—The Hierophant	Tradition/Organizing/Teacher
6—The Lovers	Decisions/Partnership/Trust
7—The Chariot	Victory/Dominance/Control
8—Strength	Fortitude/Overcoming Obstacles
9—The Hermit	Wisdom/Personal Growth/Guide
10—The Wheel of Fortune	Progress/Opportunity/Good Luck
11—Justice	Objectivity/Balance/Fairness
12—The Hanged Man	Transition/Activity Suspended
13—Death	Change/Turning Point/Cleansing
14—Temperance	Harmony/Blending Ideas/Inspired
15—The Devil	Freedom/Instincts/Desires
16—The Tower	Shocking Event/Sudden Change
17—The Star	Hopes Obtainable/Opportunity
18—The Moon	Heed Instincts/Cycles
19—The Sun	Happiness/Achievement/Success
20—Judgement	Reward/Renewal/Accountability
21—The World	Good Conclusion/Wholeness

Minor Arcana

Card	Pentacles	Swords	Wands	Cups
Ace	Prosperity	Victory	Creativity	Fulfillment
Two	Changes	Tensions Ease	New Venture	Partnership/ Love
Three	Celebrity	Unknown/ Separation	Career News	Celebration
Four	Security	Recuperation	Rewards	Reassessment
Five	Financial Worries	Lessons Learned	Competition/ Strife	Useless Regrets
Six	Generosity/ Gift	Leaving Troubles	Public Acclaim	Nostalgia/ Pleasure
Seven	Impatience	Strategy/ Cunning	Valor/ Advantage	Many Choices
Eight	Commercial Skills	Dilemma/ Patience	News Coming Fast	Turning Point
Nine	Accomplish- ment	Anxieties/ Worries	Strength/ Readiness	Wishes Fulfilled
Ten	Wealth/ Stability	Turning From Trouble	Stress/ Oppression	Recognition/ Joyful
Page	Diligent Work/ Study	Ready for Action	Restless/ Resourceful	Creative Inspiration
Knight	Propitious Occasion	Swift Action	Seeking Adventure	Opportunity
Queen	Plans Realized	Perceptive	Practical/ Optimistic	True to Own Feelings
King	Business Leader	Legal Authority	Professional Helper	Reliable Arts/ Sciences

Black Mirror Scrying

The black mirror is another excellent divination tool, used like a crystal ball for scrying or used as a ritual tool in meditations. As usual, you need to ground and center before using this item, decide what you want to explore, and perhaps light candles set at either side of the mirror, and incense behind the mirror as desired. This tool is used by gazing into the blackness without losing your focus.

Blink as necessary, allowing the mirror to fog over in your vision, then project into the mirror the thought of what you want to see: future events, specific events, past lives, ancestors, and so forth. The blackness of the reflection opens the way to other worlds with ease, and so meditation is a popular use for the black mirror.

When you are finished with your travel, scrying, or meditation, ground the excess energy and take some refreshment.

Mirrors of black glass are very expensive, but there is an easy way to create your own. Using a picture frame that can stand up, you remove the glass of the frame, wash and dry it, and you are ready to turn it into a mirror. The frame may be large or small enough to hold in the palm of your hand. When the process is completed, you will want to keep the mirror covered in a black cloth or in a black bag when not in use. Part of the process includes drawing a bindrune, which will allow passage between the worlds with balance, and offer magical protection, clear sight, power, and success. The herbs that are added at the back of the mirror will maintain grounding through Elemental Earth for divinations, meditations, and allow for astral travel from a solid foundation.

Making a Black Mirror

A mirror is only a piece of glass with one side coated or painted to keep light rays from passing through, which is then reflected back to the viewer. Take a piece of circular glass and wash it with spring water. Dry it and let it sit in the moonlight during a Full Moon and then during a Dark Moon. Next, paint the back of the glass with a glossy black enamel and let it dry. When using a photo frame, the backing comes with the frame, and you can then draw the bindrune on the inside of the backing (the part that will rest against the glass). Set the painted glass in the frame so the unpainted side faces out, place the herbs on the back of the glass, and set the cardboard backing in place, secure with the provided tabs, and seal at four points with black candle wax.

If you are not using a photo frame, then cut out a piece of black felt to fit over the painted back of the glass and glue it into place. Another method of construction using just glass rather than a photo frame is to paint black enamel in the center of a silver aluminum foil cut to fit the glass. While the paint is still tacky, but not wet, add a clear glue to the foil rim. Lay the painted foil against the clean glass and carefully press it onto the glass. This leaves a silvery edge around the mirror. After this dries, do the bindrune on a piece of paper and place with herbs on the back of the mirror, then cut and glue black felt to the back of the mirror to avoid scratching or scraping the foil and paint. This tool should also be consecrated in the usual method as shown in chapter 3. To retain the focus of the energies, only use the mirror in magical workings.

Bindrune and Incantation

Draw the runes so they form one image on the backing to be laid against the mirror or on a piece of parchment to be laid on the mirror before gluing a felt backing on, stating the function of the rune while drawing it. Draw Daeg. Use the right portion of that rune to form the top portion of Sigel. Use the left lower part of Daeg to form half of Ken. The top (arrowhead) of Tyr is formed from the bottom of Daeg. Use the right side of the arrowhead of Tyr for the protrusion on Thorn, passing the stem of Thorn through the center of Daeg. Finish with Eoh formed from the bottom right of Daeg, the stem of Tyr, and hooked off at the bottom.

ᛞ   DAEG for working between the worlds

ᛋ   SIGEL for wholeness and vitality

ᚲ   KEN for opening energy

ᛏ   TYR for success

ᚦ   THORN for protection

ᛇ   EOH for channel opened and sigil bound

Herbs and Incantation

When the paint is dry and the bindrune is ready, add a pinch of herbs (mugwort, elderflower, and lavender) to the back of mirror as it lies in the frame (pronounce *Sidhe* as "shee"):

> *I bless thee, mugwort for divination, thou elder-flower for blessing me, lavender for Otherworld and working with the Sidhe, with blessings given and received, this mirror now empowered be!*

Immediately cover the mirror with the inscribed backing from the picture frame, or place the inscribed paper on the mirror back and cover with the felt backing.

Crystal Ball and Other Stone Scryings

Any size sphere of natural quartz crystal, man-made lead crystal, glassy obsidian, fluorite, labradorite, amethyst, or any other stone that attracts you and seems willing to work with you is suitable for scrying. The ball may have bubbles or other flaws, and these can be used to aid in focusing. If the ball is clear, then you will direct your focus into the center of the ball.

Wash the crystal ball or other scrying tool in cooled mugwort tea, and use the tool consecration ritual. Then cover the ball with a black, purple, or green cloth when not in use. You can familiarize yourself with the energy or spirit of the crystal to work productively together by spending some time meditating on making contact with the indwelling entity while gazing into the ball. As usual, ground and center before using the crystal ball, ground after you finish, and take some refreshment.

To use the scrying ball, focus on the largest bubble, flaw, or center of the ball. As with the black mirror, you do not want to let your vision blur, so blink as necessary to stay focused. Think about what you want to see, then relax and let the ball become cloudy or smoky. You do not need to force a vision, but stay focused, let the cloudiness happen, and let the vision come to you. The vision will most likely be clear, unfolding within the area of focus, moving like a motion picture in color when you first start crystal gazing, and later there may be sounds and aromas. As you progress with this type of scrying, you may even depart through the crystal, seeing it all around you, then pass into other worlds. This tool, like the black mirror, is good for travel to Underworld and Otherworld, but it is also useful for seeing the present in some other location, or seeing the future.

The Pendulum

Pendulums are made with a string or chain attached to a weight made of anything from a button to a piece of metal, quartz, amethyst, lapis lazuli, or wood. These items are popular and can be found ready-made in most New Age stores and catalogs. The string or chain should not be longer than your forearm, so you can hold it without it touching a table top when suspended. The easiest way to use one is to rest your bent elbow on a table top, with the pendulum string or chain held between the thumb and forefinger of your hand so that the pendulum falls free. Focus into the center of the pendulum and mentally project into it the word, "Stop" and it should stop all movement. Ask a "Yes" or "No" answer type of question to which you already know the answer, such as, "Did I drink coffee this morning?" and watch to see which way the pendulum moves. It will move in a circle or in a line, so one of these means "Yes" and the other means "No," but it varies with the user, hence the need for a question. Once you see how the pendulum moves, you will know which is "Yes" and which is "No." Always tell the pendulum to stop between asking questions to end the current motion and prepare the pendulum for the next response. Some people make or buy a pendulum board with other answer options on it, but the pendulum needs to be swung over these options first as you explain to it what the words mean. This is called *programming*, and then you can use the pendulum with the board. A pendulum may also be used suspended in midair by one hand, and usually the other hand should be placed under it to create an energy loop.

Using the Runes

Runes are drawn, painted, or inscribed on small stones, clay tiles, slips of wood, pebbles, small crystals, etc. Again, this tool should be consecrated, then stored in a dark pouch. Handle the bag of runes while focusing on a question, then reach into the bag and pull out the number of runes needed for a spread. Lay the runes face up as they arrive out of the bag upright or reversed. You can also pull just one rune every morning for an idea of what to expect during the day. While runes may be used as alphabetical letters, particularly for inscribing your tools with your magical name, they are also used for their divinatory meanings in rune castings and spell work. You can draw runes on paper, or inscribe them in the wax of candles prior to spell casting to focus the desired energies into the magical work. Here is the list of runes with their magical interpretations, not all of which have a reversed meaning because of their design, and those colors most favorable to the rune should you want to inscribe a candle with a rune in order to meditate on the properties of the rune, or as an aid in coordinating your color choices for spell work:

Name	Sign	Letter	Meaning	Color
Osa	ᚠ	[OE]	the God; good fortune; favorable outcome (R) dubious outcome; change in fortune	green/white
As	ᚨ	[AE]	ancestor; signs; gain ancient wisdom (R) sense of futility; blocked by inhibitions	indigo/ purple
Beorc	ᛒ	[B]	Goddess; fertility; growth; beginnings (R) nurturing or new effort needed for growth	white/green
Daeg	ᛞ	[D]	daybreak; between the worlds; breakthrough	pale violet
Eh	ᛗ	[E]	movement; safe journey; progress; changes (R) movement or progress stymied	blue
Feoh	ᚡ	[F]	material wealth; fulfillment; ambition satisfied (R) frustration; lessons learned; doubtful situation	green
Gefu	ᚷ	[G]	union; partnership; love; gifts; self-confidence	pink/red
Eoh	ᛇ	[Z]	a channel; action; Otherworld communication	indigo/ purple

Name	Sign	Letter	Meaning	Color
Haegl	ᚼ	[H]	hail; limits/disruptions; awakening	white/blue
Is	ᛁ	[I]	ice; immobility; rest period; stop slander	white/silver
Gera	ᛃ	[J]	year; harvest; rewards; actual results from work	white/green
Ken	ᚲ	[K/C]	transforming fire; opening energy; fresh start (R) old-fashioned; dated; outmoded by growth	white/gold
Lagu	ᛚ	[L]	fluidity; water; psychic power; intuition; vitality (R) heed instincts; overreaching induces failure	blue/violet
Mannaz	ᛗ	[M]	Self; self-improvement; cooperation; meditation (R) blocking own progress; hindered by bad habits	indigo/violet
Nyd	ᚾ	[N]	constraint; self-control; conquer obstacles	white/blue
Ing	ᛝ	[NG]	the Horned God; fertility; family; completion	indigo
Ethel	ᛟ	[OE]	possession; home; social status; acquisitions (R) need to depart from old ways	white/gold
Perth	ᛈ	[P]	destiny; hidden forces; sudden luck; initiation (R) tied to the past; period of testing	blue/green
Rad	ᚱ	[R]	travel; quest; find what is sought; attunement (R) delicate relationships require care	blue/violet
Sigel	ᛋ	[S/Z]	wholeness; healing; energy; power	orange/gold/red

Name	Sign	Letter	Meaning	Color
Tyr	↑	[T]	victory; success; courage; favorable outcome (R) action ill-timed; questionable motives	white/gold
Thorn	Þ	[TH]	protection; gateway; foes neutralized; defense (R) hasty action is ill-advised	black
Uruz	ᚾ	[U]	strength; physical health; courage; promotion (R) need to be aware of opportunities	green/brown
Wyn	ᚹ	[W]	joy; comfort; happiness; harmony; love (R) slow results from labors; complications	pink/yellow
Eolh	ᛉ	[EA]	elk; protection; friendship; going unnoticed (R) immoderate actions; intemperate associates	white
Wyrd	[ ]	[—]	unknowable fate; destiny; cosmic influence	black/white

Rune Spreads

There are different patterns in which to lay out runes. You should use a white cloth for the reading or you may purchase or make a rune board and decorate as desired. Here are some examples of rune spreads:

1. Lay out
   1 = overview of situation
   2 = challenge
   3 = course of action needed
   4 = options and choices
   5 = evolved situation or outcome

2. Lay out 1-2-3: all upright means "Yes," all reverse means "No"; partial is "Iffy"

3. Lay out 1-2-3: 1 = present; 2 = action needed or likely; 3 = result

4. Lay out 1-2-3: 1= background; 2 = present; 3 = future

5. Lay out

		6			1 = past
		5			2 = present
3			1		3 = future
		2			4 = foundation or heart of the matter
		4			5 = obstacles or challenges
					6 = outcome or new developing situation

7

Witchcraft for Daily Living

Broom Closet: In or Out?

Witches have historically been quiet and unobtrusive—it was a matter of survival— but today the option of being in or out of the broom closet is a personal choice. The laws against Witchcraft have been repealed in most countries, and there is a gratifying resurgence of the Old Religion occurring in many places around the world, including Finland and Russia. In the United States, the estimate of 100,000 practicing Pagans/ Witches (although, granted, not every Pagan is a Witch) from the 1980s has been revised a mere twenty years later to nearly six million, and there are more people involved in the Old Ways every day. Children are being born into Pagan families, raised celebrating the Esbats and Sabbats, high-school students are wearing pentacles and challenging in court those school administrators who order them not to—and winning. The Internal Revenue Service and the *Military Chaplain's Guide* both recognize Wicca as a religion. As a result of this, Witches are becoming much more visible. The backlash is certainly out there, but the Constitution and civil laws endorse the freedom of religion. Breaking the law is not a religious prerogative, and while smaller, local courts may be reluctant to recognize the rights of people to exercise their free will and reject mainstream religions, the appeals system seems capable of resolving issues in a manner that reflects reason rather than hysteria.

Even so, how a Witch functions in modern society varies according to the person and the circumstances. There are some who make vows to be out in the open, announcing their presence to the community with pentacle jewelry, lots of black clothing, cloaks, and makeup, while others blend in with everyone else, moving unnoticed through the work day, but still feeling the spiritual connection to Nature. What it is that being a Witch means to you and how you decide to approach Witchcraft is a personal decision. Clothes and jewelry do not make a Witch, but if you are drawn to certain attire, then that is between you and the Divine of Nature. If you feel you want to grow your hair long, by all means do so. The important thing to remember is that feeling witchy is more than dress up and going for a natural look of long hair and unshaven skin. Witchcraft is *not* a cult full of rules for dress and appearance; it is *not* a regimen with severe dietary restrictions; and it is *not* a program of austere asceticism nor one of ostentatious display. What Witchcraft *is* depends upon your personal approach to Nature and communion with the Divine, whether directly or through the Elementals and Nature, and everything else from appearance, diet, exercise, to decoration and display may be your personal expression, but has little bearing on your connection to the Earth. Everyone has to decide how much or how little this personal spirituality will be coordinated with the paradigms of the surrounding society and culture.

A Witch is usually aware of the feelings of other contiguous people encountered during the average workday. Members of many religions state they accept the idea of free will and personal choice in making a commitment to their beliefs, but in Witchcraft, free will and choice is a major consideration and a matter of respecting the right of others to reject the path of Nature. The option to refuse to participate in a Nature religion is not met with a determination to convince, but this is often how mainstream religions react to having people not accept their views, and this should be a consideration when deciding whether or not to be open in public about your spiritual path.

Witches are not proselytizers, but feel that their paths are found through personal decision and a desire for connection with Nature and the Divine. There is a fine line when interacting with members of a society that has relatively little understanding for a spirituality that differs from the mainstream. Because a Witch is more connected to the psychic emanations of others, there should be a feel for how others will react to what is said and done. With this in mind, you do not want to blast another person's world view nor do you want to impose your views on others. By the same token, you do not need to feel pressured to adopt a world view or belief system you are not drawn to or do not accept. Problems with the work place, school, or neighborhood can be addressed by what you are willing to ignore or what you feel is appropriate for your situation. If the workplace has a holiday party, you can feel comfortable with this by seeing it in light of the Sabbat being represented, such as Yule for Christmas, Samhain for Halloween, Mabon for Thanksgiving, and Ostara for Easter (which is the Saxon name of the Goddess of Spring, anyway). Most people are unaware that the holidays of the modern religions are derived from those of the Old Religion, and while the Witch is very much aware, there is no need to create hostility in the work or school environment by pointing this out. Some Witches do make their spirituality known in order to take special days off from work, such as Samhain on October 31, but they make it clear that they are available to work on mainstream holidays such as Christmas (being three days after Yule). Again, the Witch walks gently, trusting intuition and the Divine. If you feel you are invited to discuss your personal viewpoints, be aware that not everyone who seems open-minded really is when the subject of Witchcraft comes up. Open minds are known to suddenly snap shut when the issue discussed is quite different than expected, and some people like to lure information from others by appearing solicitous only to turn on their victims once the details are out in the open. Be careful who you trust, and remember that some mainstream beliefs align Witches with evil and advocate that Witches should be killed. Fortunately, civil law takes precedence over religious dictums in most countries, and murder is still murder. Keep in mind, though, that there are a few countries where religious law surpasses civil law, and in such lands, a Witch who is known is not safe.

When dealing with family members and associates who you have reason to suspect may not be wildly thrilled to learn you have decided to make Witchcraft your spiritual path, it is better to walk with kindness and understanding. Not everyone hears the gentle voice of the Goddess nor feels the strong embracing arms of the God, but that does not make those people less a part of the Earth and of Nature. Everyone walks their own path, and no matter how many people are around them, they walk it alone—as do you. That is the way of life. By all means, surround yourself with as many like-minded friends as you care to, but stepping on the beliefs and rights of others to find their own path is not part of the Craft. Nor do you need to impose yourself on others. Your own calm self-confidence will speak more than any pronouncement, and you will be able to maintain a balance of the energies around you without aggravating them into tense situations. Witchcraft is not about trying to impress others, but it is about personal responsibility and unity with Nature.

There are some guidelines that may make the transition easier for you and your family. You should have a fairly good idea of how your family members feel about modern Witches—but if not, you could bring the subject up in casual conversation to find out how different members of the family think. It would not be a good idea to suddenly announce your decision to follow the Old Religion without at least a little preparation for both the rest of your family and yourself. With friends and coworkers, you could see how they react to simple matters, but if someone refers to every unpleasant person as a witch, you can guess that person's reaction if you announced yourself as one while demanding a change in the person's habits. Insensitive people are generally that way for reasons they may not understand themselves, and creating an atmosphere of hostility is not a goal of Witchcraft.

In Witchcraft, one person's style of practice usually differs in some way from that of another, but that is because of personal attunement and choice. Part of living day to day as a Witch means realigning your thinking to one of patience and acceptance of your fellow humans. There are some Witches who refer to non-Witches as *cowans* or *mundanes*, but these terms were gleaned from the early days of science-fiction conventions, and it is always dangerous to start labeling others simply because their perspective differs from yours. Besides the conceit implied, there are many people of various religious backgrounds who also appreciate Nature and see the Divine in the living Earth, and it is a disservice to the variety of Nature to fail to acknowledge the diversity of paths. Some people have natural tendencies to Witchcraft that they are not willing to admit, but function instead within their world view. The Witch moves softly upon the Earth and among the residents therein, and this includes other humans. Even when the Old Religion flourished in Europe, not everyone was what today is called a Witch. The Wise Ones of old stood apart from their own society and were seen as people who were in greater attunement with the Earth and the energies of the life cycles. They were called upon to give advice, perform magical work and healings for the benefit of the community, and lead in the celebrations, the turning of the seasons, and the honoring of the Divine.

Affirmations

Witches today recognize the cycles of life and of the Earth, the Sun, and the Moon, and it is normally part of daily life that there is some kind of affirmation of personal unity and peace with Nature and the Universe. By greeting the Sun or noting the phase of the Moon, by speaking with the creatures inhabiting your part of the Earth, by watching the stars at night and the clouds during the day, by taking enjoyment from the variety offered with each changing season, you are connecting with the enveloping arms of Nature so that every day is a sacred day. Whether you celebrate an Esbat or Sabbat or not, your life is focused in feeling and being part of what is happening at the moment. This sense of living in the present does not preclude opening a savings account or getting car and medical insurance, however. Things may certainly be done with a temperate approach. Each day for the Witch brings new awareness or gentle affirmation of the connection with the ancestors, the Divine, and Nature, opportunities for talking with the beings visible and invisible who populate all the surrounding worlds and planes of existence, giftings of bread and milk for the Fair Folk, and practicings of little spells such as for slowing time to avoid being late to work, extending the green traffic light, getting a bonus or pay raise, and being safe and protected.

Everyday life takes on new meaning, so that from morning to night the influence of Nature, the Elementals, and the Divine are evident. Making a daily affirmation as you look into the mirror in the morning (or evening) reminds you of how special you are, and of what you are—a Witch who is proud and joyful of the singular path that has been chosen. You are one with Nature and the Divine; you are alive and immortal. Smile at yourself and let your inner radiance shine through. Create your own affirmation—one that reminds you of the happiness and light you have found and embraced. Here is an example of an affirmation you can do first thing in your day, upon rising, in front of the bathroom mirror:

Daily Affirmation

Perform this during morning and/or evening daily as desired in front of a mirror, with incense or candlelight as desired. While gazing at your image in the mirror, ground and center, clearing out any static or chaotic energy within, then make the sigil of the pentagram in the air in front of you:

I am a Witch! I call out to you, Lady and Lord of Nature, and I hold you both in honor by remembering that Love is the Law and Love is the Bond! I know that I am one with all the things of the Earth and the Sky. My kin are the trees and the herbs of the fields; the animals and stones through the seas and the hills. The fresh waters and deserts are built out of you, and I am of you and you are of me. Let this day be free from strife and fear, that only joy and love come near. With blessings given and received, I walk in peace in word and deed, for I am a Witch. So Mote It Be!

Since rituals may be as simple or as complex as you like, a Daily Affirmation can be shortened to stating what is in your heart, such as:

I am a Witch! I am part of the Earth and the Universe, and I walk in unity with beings visible and invisible, one with the Elementals and one with the Lady and Lord of Nature. Where I walk, they walk, and where I am, they are. Let my example today speak well of the beauty of my path, for I am a Witch! So Mote It Be!

For something more direct, which can be thought or spoken whenever needed:

> *Lady and Lord of Nature, Elemental kith and kin, I*
> *call upon you to be with me today, guiding me in all*
> *things and protecting me from all harm. So Mote It*
> *Be!*

These are a few examples of the type of affirmation you can start your day with, but certainly you are free to create one that reflects the feelings of your heart.

Should you desire to cleanse and bless your home on a daily basis, you can perform a daily blessing at your altar by lighting incense and calling upon the Elementals and the Lady and Lord of Nature to also bring peace and harmony to you during the day.

Daily Blessing

Perform during: morning or evening on any day as desired

Materials: incense with a sage, lemony, or lavender aroma, or use a sage and sweetgrass incense bundle; incense holder; matches

Spell casting: Facing your altar at the North, ground and center, clearing out any static or chaotic energy within; light the incense and move it through air to make the sigil of the Solar Cross and the Lunar Spiral. Next make the sigil of the pentagram in the air with the incense smoke at the North, then at the East, at the South, at the West, and return to the North, setting the incense on the Altar:

> *I call upon the Lord and the Lady of Sun and Moon,*
> *to cleanse and bless this day and room. That as I*
> *will, So Mote It Be!*

Envision the smoke reaching out to all corners of the home, blanketing the energies therein with soothing gentleness:

> *Let this day be free from strife and fear; let only*
> *joy and love come near. With blessings given and*
> *received, I walk in peace in word and deed. That*
> *as I will, So Mote It Be!*

Another easy type of daily affirmation is to light a candle at your altar or a shrine you have created in your home. The shrine can have a shell for the Goddess and a horn for the God, or seasonal leaves and flowers can be set on either side of the candle holder. Lighting a small votive candle or a scented candle in a jar becomes a little reminder of the light of the Goddess and the God, and of the Elementals: the wick and solid wax represents Earth, the scent represents Air, the flame represents Fire, and the melting wax represents Water.

Living with Witchcraft

As you proceed through your day, notice how things relate to the Elementals, and look for symbols in the clouds, and speak to the creatures, plants, and stones of your surroundings. Never be hesitant about asking the Divine for something, for they will provide—but once you have asked and received, do not then reject the response. Be certain what it is you want before you ask, for to turn down what you have requested when it arrives is considered bad manners. When dealing with the Fair Folk, the matter of manners is especially important, so be sure you do not say a dismissive thank you to them, but instead express your joy at their gifts, your appreciation for their thoughtfulness, and the appropriateness of the item. Leaving a simple gift of milk and a cookie outside during the Full Moon for the Other People will bring their blessing to your home and surroundings.

In the comfort of your own home, there are a number of ways to enhance the flow of positive and protective energies. Hanging a braid of garlic bulbs or onions in the kitchen looks perfectly normal and decorative, but is actually a powerful protection charm that absorbs negativity. Never use the garlic or onion from the hanging garland in your cooking, but at the end of a year, toss it out and replace it with a fresh one—most grocery stores carry these braids in the fresh vegetable section. Another unobtrusive protection charm that also draws prosperity to the home is a cinnamon-scented broom hung by the entrance door. These brooms are dark brown in color, and are considered a decorator item, but are usually found in grocery stores and gift shops in the autumn. The broom can be embellished up with protective dried herbs suggested by your list of herbal correspondences, and with any other type of protection amulet you might want to create, such as an herbal pouch. Herbal wreaths make terrific decorations as well, and offer peace and harmony in a home without drawing attention to their magical function. Much of what is associated with country decor has associations to Witchcraft simply because the farms were the last areas brought under conversion; thus the old ways remained stronger there. The horseshoe on the outside of the house, over a door with the open end upright, is another protection charm that wards negative energies from entering a home. Add a few sprigs of the appropriate dried herbs, and you have strengthened and given greater focus to the purpose of the charm. A circle of mugwort or rosemary set onto a branch of the tree in the yard is a charm for protection as well as way of honoring a tree. Placing wind chimes on the porch in front of the door will scatter negativity before it can enter the house, especially if the chimes are reflective like the old-fashioned ones of glass. Light and musical tones will not annoy the Fair Ones, while the cheerful tunes played by the wind will remind you that Elemental Air is ever about you and able to carry your wishes off with a breeze.

Having plants around the house not only adds color and cheer, but also brings the power of the *devas*, or plant spirit energies, within for security and calmness. The magical atmosphere of your home may be augmented by the placement of natural objects such as stones, fossils, crystals, and wood items around the rooms. Doing a cleansing before moving in, or once a year afterward, helps to keep positive and beneficial energies present while removing the negative and baleful energies. Burning incense in the house periodically will also cleanse the atmosphere, draw beneficial energies, and amplify the spiritual essence of the home. Some people like to carve or draw protective symbols at locations around the house, but if living in a rental unit, this might be difficult. Hanging a decorative symbol on a wall or in an unobtrusive place may be a better way for invoking the protective energies without damaging the woodwork. You can also anoint the door jams with a protective essential oil or set a garlic clove or bay leaf in the corner of the threshold, and depending on the size of your residence, you could place some of your Craft items discreetly around the rooms to energize the house and boost the spiritual atmosphere. Choosing a color scheme according to the correlation of the colors with magical purpose can add to the magical feel of your home when doing interior decorating. Leaves, flowers, clouds and waves in wallpaper, colors of the Elementals in various rooms, all emphasize the energies of Nature. House-cleaning can become a magical process by adding herbs or essences of lavender, rosemary, or orange blossom to the laundry water, to the water used to wash the floors, or to sachets placed in the clothes drawers.

Protection pouches can be made for the automobiles, or carried in a purse or briefcase. Stones and crystals may be selected for their corresponding properties and worn as pendants, earrings, bracelets, and rings, placed in window sills and door jams, or carried in the pocket or purse. You can also create a personal shield through visualization and this can be extended over the vehicle you are in for protection. Such shields can also be created for the workplace, the home, and yourself for particular goals— to draw money or business, for protection, peace, security, to attract love, and soothe irritability.

Creating a shield through visualization is another daily use of Witchcraft. By *seeing*, or *imagining*, yourself or an area surrounded by an impenetrable bubble you are actually raising and moving protective energies through thought. The more detailed your picture the clearer the shield is to your mind, and after a few uses, it will be easier to erect the shield at a moment's notice. The more a shield image is used, the more energy it gathers quickly for defense and protection. You can see the shield as reflective blinds that you can snap shut against outside influences at will. Or, you could see yourself surrounded by a sphere of bright light that repels negative energies. Whatever makes sense to you and gives you a feeling of insulation and protection will work. You keep the shield at rest until you need it, or you can surround yourself in degrees of shielding. Too much protective shielding all the time may make you appear remote and inaccessible to other people, while too little may allow unwanted influences to come closer than you want. None at all may make you appear vulnerable and weak to others, while too much energy aimed at accomplishing a goal may make you appear overbearing.

As you work with energy and shields, you will begin to understand the different amounts of energy needed for your situation. You can create shields that attract particular energies, such as success, prosperity, and friendship, or that offer comfort to those who are upset around you. Add a tint to your clear shield to promote the qualities associated with the color, such as green for money, yellow for creativity, and pink for friendship. With shields and color, you can appear to others as an island of tranquillity in the midst of a storm, be it office politics or family quarrels.

Some people seem to have an aura of safety or confidence around them, and this is from conscious or unconscious energy manipulation and shield building, but one that is consciously created affords more solid and stable protection. Many people deliberately work at creating their persona, and this is a type of magical shielding being used through psychology. There are many Witches who have found correlations between some aspects of psychology and Witchcraft, and they take advanced studies in this field to become licensed psychologists. This does not mean that all the debated or accepted aspects of psychology actually relate to Witchcraft, but there are some that do.

All these examples are ways of bringing Witchcraft into your daily life and surroundings. You learn to see the Elementals and the Divine in all things and come to know that they are always with you. You lose the ability to hate, or the need to prove yourself or compete, because you become secure in who you are and what you do with or without the endorsement of others. When you speak to the Elementals and the Divine of Nature, they speak to you, and nothing else really matters. As you progress on your path in Witchcraft, new insights will open to you and you will discover further fields of creativity and methods of expression. The Craft is a living path, one in which the Witch grows through experience. To practice the magics of Witchcraft is to learn and to expand personal knowledge and connection with the Divine of Nature.

Following Your Own Path

There are any number of spells that a Witch can construct using the basic information and correlations presented in this work. All you have to do is decide what it is you want to accomplish, compare your supplies on hand with the lists of correspondences to select what suits your needs, and draw the materials together in the manner of your choosing. Merely calling upon the Elementals to aid you while in heavy traffic to ward off accidents, or for holding off of a downpour until you get indoors, or for finding a desired item on the store shelf when it was not previously there are examples of little spells that a Witch tosses off during a normal day's routine. Yet even something so simple becomes an opportunity to practice the Craft through living it. For the Witch, every aspect of the day is a magical moment, waiting to be dipped into or simply acknowledged with a smile or quickly raised eyebrow. Spells taken from published books of magical incantations and activities should be looked at as a guide from which you can then add a little something of your own personality to make it relevant. In all things, when you are uncertain or have questions and need direction, you have only to ask the Elementals for their assistance and put your trust in the Lady and the Lord of Nature.

As you practice Witchcraft, you become more aware of your surroundings and feel the flow of energy around you. You become more alive and vitally involved with the world because you take the time to look and experience rather than let yourself fall into a dull routine. If you realize that you have lost some of that essential gift of life, or have missed the drama of life in the trees, on the ground, in the air, and in the waters around you, then you know to take the time to meditate, to reconnect through a quiet walk in Nature or puttering in the garden to recharge your personal psychic batteries. Awareness comes from deliberately opening your senses and consciousness to your surroundings, and allowing your subconscious to receive information. You are able to utilize the energies around you, and so you must practice becoming alert to their presence through paying attention to your environs. But you must do this with a sense of respect for these energies.

Being careful about who you discuss your Craft with is important, not only for your own welfare, but for the spell crafting you do. Negative responses from those to whom you confide will throw chaotic energies at the spells you have carefully worked, so the old adage of silence is still a good one when dealing with the volatile energies of spells, charms, and other such magical undertakings.

You do not need rituals to simply let your own energies blend and flow with those of surrounding Nature to communicate with the Divine. When you do further reading on Witchcraft and begin to build a personal library, by all means try out different techniques and find out how other Witches do things, but always follow your own star—find your own path. As you follow your own path in Witchcraft, you are nevertheless joined by millions of other Witches in a special kinship that unites you with Nature, the Universe, and with one another.

The main thing to keep in mind about Witchcraft is that it is a positive, joyful celebration of life and connection with Nature and the Universe that comes from communication with the life force of Nature, with the Elementals, and with the Goddess and the God. The physical and spiritual realms are approached as equally valid and two parts of the same whole. Since the Divine resides in all things, all things are spiritual and one. If you are not happy, not having fun, and not enjoying Witchcraft, then you need to re-evaluate what you are doing. Life is not seen as a series of threats to overcome, nor as a race to a finish line with the most checks in the blocks. Witchcraft is about enjoying the life you have and living it to the fullest with the knowledge that you are loved by the Divine and that you are an integral and integrated part of Nature and the Universe. There is no need to seek the meaning of life, for the meaning is simply to live it with joy. When you follow your own star, doing that which makes you happy, the Universe opens to you and provides the means of continuing that happiness. Blessed be your feet that take you on your path.

Appendix A

Deities

Goddesses

Adraste—Goddess of Destiny

Amemet—Goddess of the Land of the West

Ana—Goddess of Plenty

Anapurna—Goddess of Plenty

Aphrodite—Goddess of Love and Beauty, but also of the Hunt

Aradia—Daughter of Diana, Goddess of the Full Moon

Ariadne—Goddess of Light

Arianrhod—Goddess of Fertility and Life Passage; Goddess of the Full Moon

Artemis—Huntress Goddess of Wildlife, Fertility, Children and Young Girls

Artemis of Ephesus—Goddess as the Great Mother

Astraea—Goddess of Justice

Asthoreth (Astarte)—Horned Goddess of Fertility and Love; Goddess of War

Bendis—Goddess of the Dark Moon, Wisdom, the Underworld, and Witches

Brigit—Goddess of Fertility, Healing, Skills, and Poets

Cerridwen—Goddess of Magic, Wisdom, the Underworld, Transformation

Cybele—Goddess of the Earth (called Ma) and Underworld

Danu—Mother Goddess, Goddess of Abundance

Demeter—Goddess of Fertility, Crops, and Fruitfulness

Diana—Goddess of the Moon, Children, Wilderness, and Witches

Diti—Goddess of Wishes Granted

Epona—Goddess of Horses and Abundance

Fortuna—Goddess of Fate and Chance

Freya—Goddess of Nature, Fertility, and Magic

Gaia—Goddess of the Earth, Earth Mother

Gerda—Goddess of Light

Harmonia—Goddess of Warrior Women

Hecate—Goddess of the Dark Moon, Magic, Wisdom, and Witches

Hulda—Goddess of the Underworld

Inanna—Goddess of the Horned Moon; Goddess of Love

Isis—Great Goddess, Mother Goddess, and Goddess of Magic

Lakshmi—Goddess of Fortune

Lola—Goddess of Gambler's Luck

Maat—Goddess of Truth and Balance

Minerva—Goddess of War, Wisdom, Crafts, and Skills

Morrigan (The)—Triple Goddess of Battle, War, and Plenty (Badb, Macha, Anu)

Nixes—Water Spirits

Norns—Three Fates

Persephone—Goddess of Corn (Wheat) and of the Underworld

Ran—Sea Goddess

Rhea—Great Mother Goddess

Rhiannon—Goddess of the Underworld

Sarasvati—Goddess of Knowledge, Poetry, Music, and Patroness of Students

Selene—Goddess of the Full Moon and Magic Workers

Sin—Fairy Women with Magical Warriors

Skadia—Mountain Goddess

Tailtiu—Goddess of the Earth

Uma Parvati—Mother Goddess, Goddess of the Earth and Fertility

Uto—Snake Goddess of Regeneration and Fertility

Vesta—Goddess of the Hearth and Home

Gods

Adonis—God of Vegetation and Rebirth

Anubis—God of the Underworld and Death Passage

Apollo—God of the Sun, Healing, Protection, and Oracles

Arawn—God of the Underworld

Attis—God of Vegetation and Rebirth (called Pa)

Baal—God of Fertility and Storms

Balder—God of Light, Vegetation, and Resurrection

Benu—God of the Sun

Cernunnos—Stag-Horned God of Nature, Fertility, Animals, and Wilderness

Chronos—God of Time

Dionysos—God of Resurrection, Cycles of Life, Wine, Divination

Dis—God of the Underworld and Riches

Eros—God of Love

Faunus—God of Herds, Crops, and Oracles

Februus—God of the Underworld

Frey—God of Nature and Fertility

Ganesha—God of Wisdom, Prosperity, and Remover
    of Obstacles

Greenman—God of Nature and the Wildwood

Hades—God of the Underworld, Wealth, and Secrets

Herne (the Hunter)—Antlered God of Nature, Gatherer of Souls

Horus—God of the Sun and Resurrection

Lugh—God of Skills, God of the Sun

Manannan mac Lir—God of the Sea and Fertility

Mimis—God of Fresh Water and Wisdom

Min—God of Fertility

Mithras—God of Warriors, the Sun, and Resurrection

Nun—God of Primal Waters

Osiris—God of the Underworld and Ressurection

Pan—Goat Horned God of Nature, Fertility, Herds, the Great All

Prometheus—God of Smithery, Crafts, and Skills

Shiva—God of Creation, Protection, Destruction, Fertility,

Silvanus—God of the Forests and Fields

Tammuz—God of Resurrection and the Underworld

Thor—God of Fertility, Thunderstorms, and Protection

Thoth—God of Writing, Wisdom, and Magic

Tyr—God of Law and Justice

Ullur—God of Justice, Archery, and Skiing

Wayland Smith—God of Smithery, Skills, and Crafting

Both

Atum—Divine Androgyne, the Great He/She

Fjorgyn—Divine Androgyne

Shiva Ardhanari—Divine Androgyne

Appendix B

Mail Order or Internet Goods and Contacts

Mail Order

AVALON (herbs, tools, supplies, jewelry, crystals, stones, tarot, books)
1211 Hillcrest Street
Orlando, FL 32803
(407) 895-7439
http://www.avalonbeyond.com

ALTERNATIVES FROM NATURE (herbs, teas, tools, gifts, supplies)
RainBear
148 South Broad Street
Lititz, PA 17543
(717) 627-1077
rainbear@herbsrainbear.com
http://www.herbsrainbear.com
http://www.witchesways.com
http://www.goddesscircle.com
Goddess Circle catalog of Witchcraft items—$4.00, send to:
Goddess Circle, P.O. Box 658, Lititz, PA 17543-0658)

BRIGIT BOOKS (books, tools, supplies)
3434 Fourth Street North
St. Petersburg, FL 33704
(727) 522-5775
http://www.brigitbooks.com

DRYAD DESIGN (statues, altar pieces, wall plaques)
37 Commercial Drive, Suite 2
Waterbury, VT 05676
http://www.dryaddesign.com

EYE OF THE CAT (herbs, tools, supplies)
3314 E. Broadway
Long Beach, CA 90803
(310) 438-3569

EYE OF THE DAY (herbs, tools, supplies)
P.O. Box 21261
Boulder, CO 80308
1-800-717-3307

LINDA RAY RESEARCH (essential oils)
Importer Essential Oils/Lotions
http://home.att.net/~LINDARAY/
LINDARAY@worldnet.att.net
(954) 583-2944

MAGIC BOOK STORE (books, herbs, tools)
2306 Highland Ave.
National City, CA 91950
(619) 477-5260

ROOTS AND WINGS (herbs, tools, supplies)
16607 Barberry, C2
Southgate, MI 48195
(313) 285-3679

SACRED SOURCE (statues, altars)
P.O. Box 163
Crozet, VA 22932
http://www.sacredsource.com

WHITE LIGHT PENTACLES/SACRED SPIRIT PRODUCTS
(tools, supplies)
P.O. Box 8163
Salem, MA 01971-8163

WITCH AND WIZARD (books, tarot, tools, herbs, supplies)
http://www.witchandwizard.com
witchandwizard@hotmail.com

EASY BREATHE (allergy herbal remedies)
http://www.easybreathe.com

Note: supplies = clothing, altar cloths, incense, candles, oils, charcoal disks, etc.

Contacts

CIRCLE
P.O. Box 219
Mt. Horeb, WI 53572
http://www.circlesanctuary.org

FLORIDA PAGAN GATHERING (FPG)
http://www.flapagan.org

SOLITARY PRACTITIONERS ASSOCIATION (SPA)
http://www.SPAssoc.info

WICCAN RELIGIOUS COOPERATIVE OF
CENTRAL FLORIDA (WRCF)
http:www.WRCF.org

Glossary

Air Elemental: representing thought, intuition, and the mind, but also the East and Sunrise, the color yellow (or red), childhood, intellect, creativity, the suit of Swords or Spades, victory, power, conflict, and the conscious mind.

Amulet: an object that may be worn for protection and is a variety of charm.

Androgyne: Image of the Divine as both male and female (Atum, Shiva Ardhanari, Mercury); a naturally born child with dual or ambiguous sexuality.

Animistic: seeing all things as having a spirit or soul, thus the Divine spirit (or the Power) resides in all things. Key phrase: *Everything is alive.*

Ardhanari: an aspect of Shiva with Shakti as "Half Male and Half Female."

Astral Plane: an energy level of existence that lies outside the physical, mental, spiritual, and etheric planes of reality.

Astral Projection: moving the spirit energy from the physical body through space and/or time to other locations while the body remains either asleep or in a trance. While the travel may be on the astral plane, it may also be manifested on the physical plane so that other people might interact with an astral projection believing it to be a physical presence, thus someone appears to be in two places at the same time.

Athame [*a-tham'me, a-thaw'me,* or *ath'a-may*]: ritual knife of Witchcraft used to direct energy in magical work and representative of the energy of the God; double-edged, generally black-handled, but any knife or knife-like object used to conduct energy for magic work may be an athame. Not used as a cutting tool, but may be used to etch symbols into candle wax or to scratch symbols on to the handle of the bolline.

Aura: energy field of multiple layers and varying colors surrounding all things that may be seen visually or sensed psychically to be understood or manipulated in magic. Gaps or holes can lead to illness and can be healed through use of crystals or other energy-moving magics as with the passing of the palms of a healer above the affected area.

Banishing Magic: type of magic that casts away something already present but undesired—*see* Repelling *and* Exorcising Magics.

Benediction: the closing of a ritual wherein blessings are given and received, and the peace of the Lady and the Lord is acknowledged.

Besom [*bes'sum*]: broom used to sweep the Circle clear of negative and chaotic energies prior to casting; may be incorporated into spellwork for fertility and astral travel.

Bindrune: a runic monogram of two to three rune symbols used as a sigil on a magical object, with the last rune drawn being the one that binds the whole.

Black Mirror: tool used for divination and meditations using a mirror of black glass or backpainted in glossy black; also name for dark objects used as mirrors, such as polished obsidian (black volcanic glass).

Blood Line Witches: Family Tradition or Hereditary Tradition Witches, whose practice has been learned from that which has been passed along within a family unit or extended family through multiple generations—not the same as Tradition Witches, which refer to those Practitioners dating from the 1940s with Gerald Gardner and later off-shoots or contemporaries of his Practice.

Blue Moon: second Full Moon in a solar month, adding spiritual energy to spells.

Bodily Energy Points: energy areas in the body at the base of spine, abdomen, stomach, heart, throat, forehead, and crown (top) of head; aligns with the chakra system of India.

Bolline [boh-leen']: practical knife of witchcraft used to cut with and inscribe objects; generally a white or brown handled knife, but some witches may utilize only one knife for the work of both the athame and bolline.

Book of Shadows (or BOS)*:* the book (or books) in which correlations are written down and referenced in the creation of spells and other magics, and in which the characteristics of a Witch's practice are given. This book will contain a code of ethics, personal philosophy, spiritual insights, meditations, lunar and seasonal and rituals (Esbat and Sabbat rituals), descriptions of tools, alphabets, recipes, rites of passage rituals, special days of observance, deity associations, and other details deemed necessary by the individual for the practice of the Craft.

Broom Closet: figurative way of describing whether a Witch prefers to keep Craft practice a secret or is more public about Craft activities, and is therefore, presumably with besom in hand, either *in* or *out* of the broom closet.

Casting the Circle: beginning of a ritual to create the Circle for magical and spiritual work to be conducted inside. The one who casts the Circle draws up energy from the Earth and balances this energy internally prior to releasing the energy to create a spherical field—*see* Ground *and* Center.

Casting Cloth: a cloth marked with designs and laid out for a divination throw, usually for ogham *fews*, but sometimes used for runes or tarot.

Cauldron: tool used to contain certain spell-crafting materials (such as a candle to be burned and melted with herbs), to hold potions and brews, and to create blessed water. It represents the fruitful and regenerative powers of the Goddess.

Ceremonial Magic: Christianized magic system created in the fourteenth–sixteenth centuries in Europe, and based on an eclectic magical world view and incorporating the Hebrew magical system of the Kabbalah, created in twelfth-century Europe, particularly in medieval Spain—*see* Grimoires.

Chakras: energy centers in the body, usually stated as root or base (genital or anal area), sacral plexus (lower abdomen), solar plexus (navel area), heart, throat, third eye (brow between and slightly above the eyes), and crown (top of the head).

Charge: directing energy into an object for a purpose; also used as a command in the directing of energy.

Charged: energized, particularly imbued with Divine blessing as with blessed water or otherwise energized or directed with a purpose during spell casting.

Charms: objects made and infused with magical energy and carried or placed to achieve a goal (such as protection, money draw, draw love and friendship)—*see also* Amulets *and* Talismans.

Circle: a ritual area created to contain raised energy that may be directed in spell work. The energy is raised through the Earth and blended within the Witch, then directed outward through the hand and wand or athame to form the Circle boundary as an encompassing sphere. When the circle is opened, the energy is returned into the Witch so that the borrowed energy may be redirected into the Earth for dissipation by touching the ground with the palms of the hands, but retaining sufficient energy for internal balance. This energy field does not act like static cling, holding negative energies in place, but is always pure and clean, simply repelling negative or chaotic energies from entering the sacred space. Also called a *Circle of Power.*

Cleansing: relieving an object of chaotic and mixed energies, often absorbed while in a store or surrounded and touched by other people. Sea salt or spring water are good for immersing an object to clear out the extraneous energies, then toss out the water or salt into which the energies have been absorbed.

Comparative Magic: "*This REPRESENTS That*" spell method in which a relationship is established between the spellcasting material and the object of the spell, so that one object acts in the place of another (used in charms and growth spells as when an energized seed is planted).

Cone of Power: energy raised within a Circle for magical use, needing to be released when at its height for effective magic to take place.

Contagion Magic: a subdivision of a generic definition of Sympathetic Magic, indicating that something of the material used in spell casting has been in contact with the subject of the spell work.

Containment Magic: type of magic that shields or protects: keeping an area secure with positive energies retained inside and negative energies held at bay; or placing a shield over the source of negative energies, thus keeping those energies confined in that area—*see* Deflection *and* Reflection Magics.

Correspondences: correlations of magical energy to items of Nature, colors, hours of the day, days of the week, symbols, alphabetic interpretations, lunar and solar phases, and other such meanings to be used in creating or interpreting magical work—see Lists of Correspondences.

Cosmic Lemniscate: the symbol of Infinity, like a number 8 on its side ∞, drawn in the air over the altar during Circle Casting to signify standing between the worlds: "I stand in a place that is not a place and in a time that is not a time."

Coven: assembly of Witches, generally adhering to agreed upon standardized procedures or those of a particular Tradition and generally having thirteen members with one being the leader as High Priest or High Priestess, although there may be two leaders, male and female, and the leadership may alternate among the members.

Covenhome: the name of a Witch's coven, such as, "Her covenhome is the Coven of the Sacred Wheel." The term has been mainstreamed since the 1970s as referring to a "church home."

Covenstead: limited area (such as a five-mile radius) for covens so that there are not overlapping territories within the same Tradition.

Craft: Witchcraft, the Old Religion of pre-Christian Europe.

Craft Name: a magical or spiritual name chosen by a Witch for working in the Craft, and may be used openly, in Pagan community settings, and in "outer court" Circles. This name may also be used as a coven name, although many covens prefer to rename someone entering their circle. If this name is unknown to other people, then it may double as the Working Name.

Cross-quarters: Sabbats of Samhain, Imbolc, Beltane, and Lughnassadh, also known as the White or Greater Sabbats, or as the Fire Sabbats for the community bonfires that were traditionally lit on hilltops.

Cup: contains the beverage used during ritual, and to symbolize the receptive and fertile womb of the Goddess; also called a chalice or goblet.

Curses: contain malevolence to the sphere of the generator of the negative energy—*see* Containment Magic.

Daoine Sidhe [Dee'nay Shee]: the Shining Ones who are the powerful folk or nobility of the Other People or Elves.

Dark Moon: representative of the Goddess as the "One Who Transforms" in her aspect of Tomb and Womb, thus a time more suited for meditation and divination than for magical work or spells.

Dark Power: generally negative or chaos energies drawn from the Dark Aspects of the Goddess and the God, which stimulate creativity and innovation.

Deflection Magic: type of magic used to defuse general malevolence and ill will of others by randomly dispersing and dissipating the negative energies—*see* Containment *and* Reflection Magics.

Deosil [Dee'o-sil or *Jesh'el]:* clockwise movement; the course of the Sun through the sky.

Deva: "Shining Ones" of Hinduism; Divine Beings and Nature Spirits.

Directive Magic:"This AFFECTS That" spell method in which energy of one object is moved to influence another. Energy is also raised, focused, directed, and sent to accomplish a goal, and this is the most commonly used in all types of magic, often in connection with Lists of Correspondences.

Drawing Down The Moon: a ritual of drawing the energy of the Full Moon into water to be blessed, but also a ritual of the Full Moon Esbat in which the spiritual energy of the Goddess is drawn within the Witch for communion and prophecy.

Drawing Magic: type of magic that brings something to the Practitioner, hence enticing and invoking an energy influence.

Dressing: putting an appropriate oil on spell items such as candles as part of a ritual consecration to prepare the object to attract and direct the energy of a spell to accomplish a goal.

Earth Elemental: representing strength, but also the North and Midnight, the color green (or black), old age, stability, wisdom, the suit of Pentacles or Coins, business, and money.

Eke Name: a coven name or "inner court" name by which a practitioner of the Craft is known within a Circle.

Elementals: the energy archetypes of the Goddess and the God expressed as individual entities and powers embodying the four elements of Earth, Air, Fire, and Water. These are emanations of Divine Power, respected and worked with in the focusing of energy, not as simple energies or servants, but as Powers. However, they are not worshipped as the dictionary definition of elementalism. Water and Earth are often ascribed to the Goddess, while Air and Fire are ascribed to the God. These categories reflect the images of Sun God and Sky God, Moon Goddess and Earth Goddess, but may also be interchanged as with an Earth God or Sea God, a Goddess of Creative Thought (Air) and Power (Fire).

Elysium Fields: Greek plain of ideal happiness and joy; paradise for the dead who lived virtuous lives without harming others, and thus correlates as a land of repose within the Underworld, known in Witchcraft as the Summerland.

Eleusian Mysteries: secret Greek religious rites honoring Demeter at the site of Eleusis each spring during which initiations into the Mysteries of Demeter took place symbolizing the annual death and resurrection of grain and vegetation; showing the relationship between the life cycles of the Earth and the people who are part of the Earth, so that all are seen as born from the seed, aging, dying, and returning into the seed to be reborn. It is known that anyone who passed through the rite was so transformed as to be changed utterly by the awareness of the immortality of the spirit. This theme is carried through in the Wheel of the Year of Witchcraft, showing the passage of the God through the cycle of the year to demonstrate the resurrection motif and show the immortality of the spirit within.

Esbat [*Es'bat*]: lunar celebrations of Witches during the Full and New Moons (last sliver of lighted Moon before the Dark Moon); often used in conjunction with spell work.

Etheric Plane: an energy level of existence not on the physical or mental plane, nor on the astral, but in between where it acts as a connecting passage.

Exorcising Magic: type of magic that casts away negative energies preventing their return, so that positive energies may enter— *see* Banishing *and* Repelling Magics.

Exorcism: aiding spirits in their death passage who may feel lost, confused, or unaware of their transition from physical into spirit form; dispersing negative energies to allow positive energies to enter.

Fairy Moon: see Sidhe Moon.

Familiar: Witch's animal or spirit helper in magical work.

Fire Elemental: representing energy and vitality, but also the South and Noon, the color red (or white), youth, ambition, drive, the suit of Wands orRods, career, and creativity.

Full Moon: lunar phase symbolizing the Goddess in her aspect of Mother, Lady of Abundance and Compassion; a time for magic and spell workings involving completion, fruition, protection, containment, honoring energies and spirits, and Drawing Down the Moon.

Greater Sabbats: those of the harvests and mythic cycles of the Goddess and the God: Samhain, Imbolc, Beltane, and Lugh nassadh; also called the White or Fire Sabbats and the Cross-Quarters on the Wheel of the Year.

Greenman: The God as Lord of the Wildwood, Lord of Nature, a revealer of mysteries and mentor to the occult student. His feast is in May, and he is associated with the May King, Cernnunos, Jack in the Green, Robin of the Wood, the Summer Lord, and the Fool card of the Tarot. He is also related to such woodland/resurrection deities as Adonis, Attis, Dionysos, Tammuz, and Silvanus.

Green Sabbats: the Quarters or Lesser Sabbats of the turning of the seasons, thus Winter and Summer Solstice (Yule and Litha) and Spring and Fall Equinox (Ostara and Mabon).

Green Woman or *Green Lady:* sylvan Goddess such as Flora, often connected to Fairy motifs such as with Greensleeves.

Grimoires [*Grim'ores,* also *Grimore'es,* or even *Grim'waws*]: from the word *grammar*; these were books of magical formulas created by Ceremonial Magicians between the twelfth and sixteenth centuries in Europe, containing elaborate Christianized magical rituals based on eclectic European Paganism and the Hebrew Kabbalah of twelfth-century Europe. These use the dichotomy concepts of Heaven and Hell, good and evil, light and dark, angels and demons, and hierarchies of celestial and infernal beings to be summoned and banished according to the will of the magician. There are names of power, lists of correspondences between objects and magical powers, seals and sigils, and other such information for the working of magic by externally commanding these energies. The term is now used also for the Witch's Book of Shadows, particularly that portion relating to magic and spell casting.

Ground and Center: releasing internal static energies into the ground through the feet or hands, then finding the calm center within, followed by drawing up strong Earth energies through the feet, pulling it up to intertwine with the personal energies to create a stronger internal energy balance as preparation for spell work. This is done to avoid depleting personal energy in Circle casting and spell work—*see* Grounding.

Grounding: touching the Earth or floor with the palms of hands after magical work to drain off excess energy in order to regain a normal internal energy balance and avoid irritability, headache, and nervousness; releasing excess energy into the

Earth upon completion of energy raising for Circle casting, ritual, meditation, spell work, and other magical workings—*see* Ground *and* Center.

Homeopathic Magic: a subdivision of the generic definition of Sympathetic Magic indicating that spell casting is conducted through the use of lists of correspondences.

Immanence: the immediacy of the Divine as at hand and present in all things.

Inhabited: companion or other spirit entity dwelling in a crystal from time to time and may be contacted through that crystal.

Karma: Hindu idea of soul destiny formed by balancing in the current life the actions of previous lives in order to facilitate a more propitious future incarnation.

Ken, Kenned, Kenning: all-encompassing sensation of *knowing* something with a certitude and acceptance that is mentally understood, emotionally felt, and psychically sensed so that there is not doubt that what is kenned, *is*. Also used to indicate penetratingly keen and instinctive insight.

The Lady and the Lord: the Goddess and the God of the Old Religion, the deities of Nature and the Universe through Whom the Power flows.

Lesser Sabbats: those of the Solstices and Equinoxes: Yule, Ostara. Litha, and Mabon, also called the Green Sabbats and the Quarters on the Wheel of the Year.

Libation: an offering to the Goddess and the God, usually the first draught of ritual beverage and the first portion of ritual food unless the ritual designates otherwise.

Light Power: generally positive and orderly energies drawn from the Light Aspects of the Goddess and the God.

Lists of Correspondences: a variety of tables kept in the Book of Shadows or Grimoire showing a correlation between items and their magical function as used in the practice of the Craft and spell casting, such as between colors, herbs, days of the week, hours of the day, and a magical intent, as when burning a green candle with mint leaves on a Thursday at the third hour after sunset for a money spell—also called Tables of Correspondences.

Lord and Lady: direct translation of many ancient names for the God and Goddess of the Old Religion, the deities of Nature and the Universe, through Whom the Power flows.

Lunar Eclipse: emblem of the Goddess in Her Dark Aspect as Crone, when she is both the Tomb and the Womb, hence, the one through whom the spirit is transformed and passed from one life to the next.

Magic: creating changes by the raising or gathering, focusing, directing, releasing, and sending of energy.

Meditation: quiet relaxation in which the mind-chatter is silenced so as to open an altered state of awareness wherein the conscious mind is subdued, allowing the subconscious functions of the mind to dominate; state of relaxation and accessibility.

Moons: there are twelve Full Moons in a year, beginning with the one in December, with even some of the common names for these Moons distributed differently according to personal and traditional preference: Oak (December), Wolf (January), Storm (February), Sap or Hare (March), Seed (April), Hare or Dryad (May), Dryad or Mead (June), Herb (July), Barley, Corn, or Mead (August), Harvest (September), Hunter's (October), and Snow (November). A thirteenth Moon creating two Full Moons in one solar month is called the Blue Moon, and when the Moon is a red or dark russet color in any month, it is called a Blood Moon, adding the energy of power and aggression to whatever is the normal name for the Moon.

Moon Phases: Waxing for beginnings and developing magics (Maiden); Full for completions, honoring energies and spirits, and Drawing Down the Moon (Mother); Waning for banishings, purgings, and exorcisms (Crone); and Dark or New for meditations and divinations (Goddess of Mysteries, the Hidden Face of the Goddess).

Mystic Moon: the Dark Moon seen as the Hidden Face of the Goddess. May be called the New Moon unless this term is associated with the last thin crescent of the Waning Moon as depicted in the Triple Goddess symbol.

New Moon: lunar phase symbolizing the Goddess in her aspect of Crone, Dark Lady, and Wisdom; a time for banishing and repelling magics. Esbat celebration held at the last visible crescent prior to the Dark Moon.

Old Religion: pre-Christian Nature religions of Europe.

Opening The Circle: ending of a ritual with the Circle being uncreated after all magical and spiritual work has been concluded within. This draws the energy field back into the person who cast the Circle for the internal energies to be brought into balance and the excess energy released through the palms of the hand by touching the ground or floor.

Otherworld: the world of the Other People, also called Elves (Sidhe), Fair Ones, and Fairies.

Pagan: Rustic or Country Dweller, hence, the name for people who retained the practices of the Old Religion during the Christianization of European cities, and now used as a name for all non-Christian religions and their adherents.

Pantheistic: all energies and matter are aspects of the Divine, thus the Divine is manifested in everything. Key phrase: *Everything is Divine.*

Pentacle: any object, amulet, jewelry, or other type of adornment or charm constructed with a pentagram (five-pointed star in a circle), but mainly drawn, carved, or engraved on a disk of wood, tile, metal, etc. as a ritual tool that is meant to represent Elemental Earth on a Witch's altar. Sometimes other symbols are included, such as those for the Horned God and the Triple Goddess, planetary sigils, and so forth. When worn as jewelry, it represents the four Elementals of Earth, Air, Fire, and Water, and Spirit, and is a religious symbol of Witchcraft.

Pentagram: a drawing, inscription, or hand motion of a five-pointed star, usually within a circle, with the points representing the four Elementals and the Spirit, generally with Air and Water on the left and right arms, Earth and Fire on the left and right legs, Spirit at the top, and the Practitioner at the Center, although the latter two images may be reversed with the Practitioner at the top and Spirit at the center, particularly in relation to spell work.

Poppet: doll figure used in magical spell casting, usually stuffed with herbs or batting, and meant to be a helper or represent someone.

The Power: the Universal energy of the Divine expressed through the Deities, the Elementals, and such cosmic bodies as the Sun, the Moon, the Earth, stars, planets, comets, and meteors. One who feels these energies and can move them is said to "have the Power" and hence is a Witch.

Power Hand: the hand a person favors, used in ritual context for the power found in the dominant hand, and thus the one through which energy is passed for magic and spell casting.

Protection Magic: a use of Containment, Deflection, or Reflection Magics.

Purgings and Releasings: lesser exorcisms that cleanse and turn away negativity or impediments, absorb negativity to be buried for grounding, and dissipating negative energies.

Quarters: Sabbats of Yule, Ostara, Litha, and Mabon, also known as the Green or Lesser Sabbats. Also the word used to describe the locations of the four Elementals for "calling the Quarters" during Circle casting when the Elementals are invoked with Earth at the North, Air at the East, Fire at the South, and Water at the West of the perimeter.

Rade: "ride"—the wild ride of the Hunter gathering the souls of the dead; the passing of the Wild Hunt or the Rade is demonstrated by stormy weather and fast moving, roiling black clouds in the sky.

Reflection Magic: type of magic that turns away negative energy, sending it back to the source; used in "return to sender" magics. S*see* Containment *and* Deflection Magics.

Repelling Magic: type of magic that casts away something that may be present or is approaching the Practitioner, hence banishing or exorcising an energy influence, with purgings and releasings being lesser exorcisms. *See* Banishing *and* Exorcising Magics.

Retribution: returning negative energy to the sender and sealing it there, usually by visualization or with the added energy of herbs.

Return-to-Sender Magic: send intentionally harmful negativity back to its originating source.

Rituals: magical or devotional ceremonies in which energy is raised for Divine communion and/or for the conducting of magic as with spell work.

Runes: old Teutonic and Norse alphabet symbols associated with magical meanings and often used as sigils in spells and other magical workings.

Sabbat [Sab'bat]: Eight holy days of Witchcraft representing four seasonal or solar celebrations and four fire or agricultural celebrations. The four solar ones are the spring and fall equinoxes, and the summer and winter solstices. The agricultural ones are the harvests of August (grains) and October (root and gourd), the lambing time of February, and the fullness of Spring in May. Some people reverse the Sabbats for the Southern Hemisphere to align with seasonal changes, others prefer to celebrate according to the traditional European dates. It is simply a matter of personal preference.

Scrying: psychic divination in which images are seen within a magical tool such as a black mirror, crystal ball, water as well as in things of Nature such as clouds, smoke, birds in flight, and so forth. Anything that lends itself as an appropriate medium can be scryed, such as with obsidian.

Seals: magical diagrams using symbols, or using the numerical equivalents for names and planets in a square, perhaps with a sigil superimposed over it.

Shadowland: Underworld realm of repose for spirits who have ended their incarnations and made the death passage. It is seen as a tranquil, dimly lit land ruled by the Lord of Shadows aspect of the God and by the Crone aspect of the Goddess and is a place where the spirit rests before moving into Summerland for revitalization and onto rebirth—*see* Summerland *and* Underworld.

Sidhe [*Shee*]: Elves, the Fairie people of Ireland, the Tuatha de Danu [*Too'a day Dan'nu*]—*see also* Daoine Sidhe.

Sidhe Moon: the second Dark Moon in a solar month, being a propitious for working with the Sidhe and adding psychic energy to magical workings.

Sigils [*Sig'el* or *Sij'el*]: a design drawn or engraved for magical power, representing a planet, aspects of the Goddess and the God, or a desired goal, using runic symbols, Witchcraft symbols and used as a focus in a magical working.

Solar Eclipse: emblem of the God in His aspects of Dark Lord, Lord of Shadows, Death, Chaos, Resurrection, Hunter, and Leader of the Wild Hunt.

So Mote It Be!: "*So Must It Be!*" given as an emphatic statement of affirmation and finality in the working of a spell, in rituals, and in portions of Circle casting and opening, sometimes prefaced with "That As I Will," and may be substituted with "It Is Done!"

Spells: magic gathered and directed in ritual to achieve a goal, thus spells are the vehicles of magical workings utilizing the movement of energy through the power of spoken word or formula, be it in a ritual, brew, charm, amulet, talisman, prayer, visualization, or crafted item created for magical purpose, generating intent into manifestation.

Summerland: the Underworld realm where the rested spirit may enjoy a paradise of light and joy, and where the spirit may remain or move on to rebirth; comparable to the Elysium Fields of the Greek worldview—*see* Shadowland *and* Underworld.

Symbols: letters, sigils, and designs used in Craft work and spells.

Symbolism: meanings and interpretations for divination images and omens.

Sympathetic Magic: "*This IS That*" spell method of Witchcraft in which the spell casting material is seen as the actual object of the spell (poppets, sigils, and seals), but also a generic term for magic under the concept of all things being connected through energy, and further subdivided between contagion and homeopathic magic techniques.

Tables Of Correspondences: same as Lists of Correspondences.

Talisman: an object such as a ring or pendant, engraved with magical symbols to bring good fortune, offer protection, ward misfortune, etc. It is a type of charm.

Tarot [*Tair'roe*]: deck of seventy-eight cards, descended from those created in India carried into northern Italy by Romany Gypsies, originally used in a game called Tarrochi in the fifteenth century and now used mainly in divination; the deck contains twenty-two archetype cards called the Major Arcana, and fifty-two cards typical of regular playing decks, plus four additional cards of Page or Princess for each of the four suits, called the Minor Arcana. In modern card decks, the Swords became Spades, the Cups became Hearts, the

Disks/Coins/Pentacles became Diamonds, and the Wands became Clubs.

Traditions: word used by Wiccan or Witchcraft denominations dating from the 1940s, with many requiring a chain of denominational initiation based on the specific Tradition's instruction, but not the same as Family Tradition or Hereditary Tradition, which are passed along within a family unit or extended family through multiple generations, and whose members may also be called Bloodline Witches.

Transference Magic: "This ENTERS That" spell method of Witchcraft in which the negative or undesired energies within one object or person are moved into another willing receptacle, often a plant, animal, or stone (such as using a grounding stone to gather negative energies, then burying it or washing it off in the sea or running water).

Triple Goddess and Triple God: the Goddess as threefold Maiden, Mother, Crone and the God as threefold Child, Father, Sage although there are variations of terms according to the mythic symbology being used, hence the Child may be a baby or youth, and the Father may be a warrior or fertility symbol such as the Horned God or Greenman.

Tuatha de Danu [*Too'a day Dan'nu*]: "The People of the Goddess Danu," Celtic name for the Sidhe or Fairie Folk of Ireland. It is Sanskrit for the Dravidic people of Sind who called the Goddess Danu, showing a connection between the Celts and the Dravidic people of India from around 3,000 years ago.

Turning of the Wheel: passage through the yearly cycle of eight Sabbats, hence, the passage of the year marked by the celebrations therein, and the following of the myth of the God as the Oak King and the Holly King, and the roles of the Goddess as Maiden, Mother, and Crone during the year.

Twin Aspects of Magic: purpose and method, with the purpose being to draw desired energy, to repel undesired energy, or to contain desired energy while warding off undesired energy; and with method being the way the energy is manipulated through either sympathetic, comparative, directive, or transference magic, or a combination of these to achieve a desired goal.

Underworld: the world where all spirits of the dead go, and may be seen as divided between a Shadowland realm of repose and recuperation, and a Summerland realm of bliss and renewal of energies.

Wand: a tool for gathering and transferring energy in the performance of magic; may be made of a branch of wood, generally the length of the forearm, from a tree selected for the type of correlation of the wood to the main type of magic conducted: oak (God focused), elder and willow (Goddess focused), and hazel (Witch and Nature focused) being popular choices. It may also be of crystal or metal tubing filled with herbs, crystals, etc. and may be wrapped with copper wire.

Waning Moon: lunar phase of the Crone for magical work and spells involving diminishment, exorcisms, repellings, and banishings.

Water Elemental: representing emotions and psychic power, but also the West and Sunset, the color blue (or gray), maturity, feelings, intuition, the suit of Cups or Hearts, love, abundance, and the subconscious mind.

Waxing Moon: lunar phase of the Maiden for magical work and spells involving initiating action, a new beginning, drawing, growth, and increase.

White Sabbats: the Cross-Quarters, Greater or Fire Sabbats of Samhain, Imbolc, Beltane, and Lughnassadh.

Witches' Rede: long version is usually summed up in the admonition "An' it harm none, do as thou wilt," the ethical law of Witches.

Widdershins: counterclockwise, or the opposite of the course of the Sun in the sky, also called *Tuathal*, meaning to unwind, and is the direction used to open a Circle that had previously been cast deosil (clockwise).

Witchcraft: foundational aspect of the Old Religion, grounded in Nature, approaching the Craft through the Elementals, the Other People, and the Goddess and the God, using herbs, natural objects, and Earth energy in spell crafting. The Divine is seen as the Lady and the Lord of the Wildwood, primarily as Earth Mother and Horned God, symbolized by the Moon and Sun, but also in their many other natural (rather than social or political) aspects, and thus the Craft is both animistic and pantheistic. The energies raised join internally with that of the Witch to be focused, directed, released, and sent to accomplish a goal. Seen as a spirituality, thus holding the word "Witch" to be honorable and spiritual, related to the Teutonic concept of *seidhr*. The term was created to distinguish non-Christian people who actively followed the Old Religion, and were also called heathens and Pagans. It may be derived from Anglo-Saxon or Middle English (Medieval time period) words meaning "a wise councilor" (Witta, pronounced *Wee'ta*), or "a clever and knowing sorcerer or magician" (Wicce, pronounced *Weetch'ee*). Some feel the word is derived from *wicker*, meaning "to bend and shape," but the actual root word is very different and had been in use much longer than the term "Witch" or "Witchcraft." In rural areas, Witches were more likely to be called by a title before the first or last name such as Mother, Grandmother, Granny, Little Mother, Father, Grandfather, Gaffer, Old Man, and so forth.

Working Between The Worlds: moving between planes of existence; between the physical world and other worlds (astral, etheric, spiritual, etc.).

Working Name: secret name chosen by the Witch for use in magical and ritual practice and never revealed to anyone. The chosen name is changed when one is bestowed on the Witch directly by the Goddess and the God in a Dedication Ritual, or at such time as when the Practitioner is united with the Divine. For Solitary Practitioners, the Working Name and the Craft Name may be the same only if they do not use it among other people, as was often the case prior to the public revival of the Old Religion.

Wyrd: unknowable fate or destiny, cosmic influence, the blank rune in divination indicating that the answer is hidden and under the power of the Divine.

Selected Books for a Witch's Library

Adler, Margot. *Drawing Down the Moon; Witches, Druids, Goddess-worshippers, and Other Pagans in America Today.* Boston: Beacon Press, 1979.

Beyerl, Paul. *A Compendium of Herbal Magick.* Custer: Phoenix Publishing, Inc., 1998.

Buckland, Raymond. *Buckland's Complete Book of Witchcraft.* St. Paul: Llewellyn Publications, 1994.

Campanelli, Pauline. *Ancient Ways: Reclaiming Pagan Traditions.* St. Paul: Llewellyn Publications, 1991.

———. *Wheel of the Year: Living the Magical Life.* St. Paul: Llewellyn Publications, 1990.

Conway, D. J. *Celtic Magic.* St. Paul: Llewellyn Publications, 1990.

Cunningham, Scott. *The Complete Book of Incense, Oils & Brews.* St. Paul: Llewellyn Publications, 1990.

———. *Cunningham's Encyclopedia of Magical Herbs.* St. Paul: Llewellyn Publications, 1989.

———. *Wicca for the Solitary Practitioner.* St. Paul: Llewellyn Publications, 1989.

Farrar, Janet and Stewart. *A Witches' Bible: The Complete Witches' Handbook.* Custer: Phoenix Publishing, Inc., 1981.

González-Wippler, Migene. *The Complete Book of Spells, Ceremonies, Magic.* St. Paul: Llewellyn Publications, 1988.

Green, Marian. *A Witch Alone.* London: The Aquarian Press, 1991.

K, Amber. *True Magick: A Beginner's Guide.* St. Paul: Llewellyn Publications, 1990.

Lust, John. *The Herb Book.* New York: Bantam Books, 1974.

Mindell, Earl. *Earl Mindell's Herb Bible.* New York: Simon & Schuster, 1992.

Moura, Ann (Aoumiel). *Green Magic: The Sacred Connection to Nature.* St. Paul: Llewellyn Publications, 2002.

———. *Grimoire for the Green Witch: A Complete Book of Shadows.* St. Paul: Llewellyn Publications, 2003.

———. *Green Witchcraft: Folk Magic, Fairy Lore & Herb Craft.* St. Paul: Llewellyn Publications, 1996.

———. *Green Witchcraft II: Balancing Light and Shadow.* St. Paul: Llewellyn Publications, 1998.

———. *Green Witchcraft III: The Manual.* St. Paul: Llewellyn Publications, 2000.

———. *Origins of Modern Witchcraft: The Evolution of a World Religion.* St. Paul: Llewellyn Publications, 2000.

———. *Tarot for the Green Witch.* St. Paul: Llewellyn Publications, 2003.

Pennick, Nigel. *The Complete Illustrated Guide to Runes.* Boston: Element Books, Inc., 1999.

Starhawk. *The Spiral Dance, A Rebirth of the Ancient Religion of The Great Goddess.* New York: Harpercollins Publishers, 1989.

Thorsson, Edred. *The Book Of Ogham: The Celtic Tree Oracle*. St. Paul: Llewellyn Publications, 1992.

——. *Northern Magic: Mysteries of the Norse, Germans & English*. St. Paul: Llewellyn Publications, 1992.

Williams, Jude C. *Jude's Herbal Home Remedies*. St. Paul: Llewellyn Publications, 1996.

Index